CRASHING STEEL

CRASHING STEEL

A PERSONAL VIEW

By
Stewart Dalton

*'A line of poplars by the riverbankside -
that is all that remains of 140 years
of metal working at Tinsley Rolling Mills'*

Wharncliffe Publishing

First Published in 1999 by
Wharncliffe Publishing
an imprint of
Pen and Sword Books Limited,
47 Church Street, Barnsley,
South Yorkshire. S70 2AS

*For up-to-date information on other titles produced under the
Wharncliffe imprint, please telephone or write to:*

    Wharncliffe Publishing
    FREEPOST
    47 Church Street
    Barnsley
    South Yorkshire S70 2BR
    Telephone (24 hours): 01226 - 734555

ISBN: 1-871647-73-8

A CIP catalogue record of this book is available from the
British Library

Cover illustration: By kind permission of the artist Stan Jackson

Printed in Great Britain by
Redwood Books, Trowbridge, Wiltshire

CONTENTS

Chapter 1

CHILDHOOD ASPIRATIONS

A SMALL CHILD GROWING UP on a Council estate in post war Sheffield, could easily be forgiven for believing that steel was the most important commodity in the world. After all it was everywhere; in the house, in the form of buckets, pans, baths, cutlery as well as being in many toys. Outside the home it was in daily use - the tram tracks, lamp standards, bus shelters, lorries and bikes - they too were made of steel, and the daily grime that invaded our lives came from the works that produced it. Steel and its associated engineering activities were the sole source of income for most working class families. The work provided the family income which paid for the rationed food, clothing and the very occasional treat.

More importantly steel had helped win the recent war which, as an alternative to 'cowboys and indians', was played out on a daily basis with the youngest of the group usually being forced to take the part of 'Jerry'. Sheffield, so we were told, had made all the big guns, bombs and battleships' armour without which we should have been helpless against the enemy. In our innocence we were as proud of Sheffield's industry as we were of either of our two local football teams, *The Blades* or *The Owls*. The steel industry permeated our lives, as well as our small lungs.

The 'Dark Satanic Mills' we sang about in morning assembly could only have been written with Sheffield in mind: our skyline was dominated by hundreds of smoking chimneys and the City lived to the constant accompaniment of steam hammers and the ring of metal meeting metal. These visible and audible reminders of the supremacy of Vulcan in his Kingdom would only vanish during Works shutdown, when those lucky enough would race off for a week at the seaside, leaving those less fortunate to venture onto Wincobank Hill and look across the smoke free Don Valley and, for perhaps the first time, see in the distance the fields toward Laughton. When in later years, Sheffield would proudly proclaim its credits as a clean air City, its detractors would churlishly publish old photographs of this smoke-filled valley - much to the annoyance of Sheffielders.

A trip to town on the tram, if possible via Attercliffe, offered the chance for a bit of train-spotting as the route took the tram alongside

Brightside Engine Sheds. The locomotive stock rarely offered anything interesting and the chance for a 'Kop', was pretty remote but an opportunity was never missed to try and underline a number in the much treasured Ian Allen handbook. Running parallel with the sheds was English Steel Corporation's Acid Siemens melting shop which in the dark, offered terrifying glimpses of molten steel being poured into ingot moulds. This was always accompanied by a display of sparks and flashes which would belittle anything to be seen on Bonfire Night. A small boy may also have been forgiven for the belief that the breed who worked in such awesome circumstances were very special. And they were; they were our dads, grandads, uncles and cousins and very, very occasionally, our mums.

Not only did the steelworks' smoke enter the lungs. 'There's nothing wrong with him; he's just got a Sheffield cough', was the frequent reply a concerned mother would get after consulting the doctor, but to the very susceptible, steel could enter the individual's psyche and a lifelong 'feeling' for it would develop. Children on the housing estates could be heard arguing, 'My dad works at ESC. It's better than Firth Browns.' Pity the child whose father's occupation was so humble as to be ignored in the daily round of squabbles. The melter, the roller, the forgeman...these were the 'worthy' occupations, not comparable in any way with the 'wimpish' occupations found outside the factories. Sheffield made things, and unless your dad's company made things needing either skill or effort, it didn't rank in the childish league table of proper jobs. The sheer hard, physical effort and long hours our fathers worked, often in poor environmental conditions, went unrecognised by the children who, with shift working, had very little of what we now call 'quality' time with their fathers, who in any case probably preferred to relax in one of the City's many pubs and working men's clubs. Not that work was left behind there, for it was a frequent and proud topic to be knowledgeably discussed at length, as their pints were consumed. The biggest ingot ever cast or the latest technique in forging would be debated in *The Fox and Duck,* as frequently as it was in any Boardroom.

Sheffield was a proud City, and its workers proud of their skills. The achievements of its industry were used to bolster morale in the post war austerity years. The production of publicity films by the very largest steel firms, portrayed a City whose skills contributed to the renewal of the country's economic prospects. The latest jet engines, aircraft, ships, cars and nuclear power all seemed to rely upon some vital component which the City had made. Sometimes, if you were especially fortunate these components might be seen on the way to their destination. Huge multi-wheeled Pickfords vehicles would haul the very largest castings or forgings at a snail's pace along the City's roads. Placards alongside the gargantuan piece of steel would indicate its dimensions, weight and ultimate use. Only Sheffield could make it...or so we thought!

Schooldays led inevitably toward the 11-plus or 'scholarship', as this interesting piece of social engineering was still known locally. If failed, parental opinion was that it would lead to a life as 'foundry fodder' or worse. Consequently, various rewards for passing were tantalisingly on offer. If all the bikes had been bought as were offered, the Raleigh factory in Nottingham would have worked extra shifts in the June of 1954. As it was, fewer bikes were obtained than places at Grammar School. Not many working class parents had any real idea of the objectives of a Grammar School education and even fewer pupils realised its implications beyond the acquisition of a uniform and a satchel. The satchel, which was often utilised as a handy weapon, allegedly should have been used to carry homework and a collection of time expired graffiti daubed textbooks to aid its completion. More often though, the well established network for 'cribbing' the time wasting evening chore, was utilised to the full'. Only rarely being compromised by an over-observant Master.

Firth Park Grammar was housed in a somewhat daunting old house, known as 'The Brushes'. Two notable industrialists had lived there in earlier times. John Booth, whom we shall come across again was one, but perhaps more famously, it was owned by C W Kayser, a scissor forger who came from Germany and was to make his fortune as a Steelmaster, far from his native Rhineland. The tower, still a notable feature of The Brushes, was allegedly built by the self-

'The Brushes' home of Firth Park Grammar School.

exiled German to remind him of home. These must have been infrequent thoughts since, according to Sheffield's pioneer of stainless steels, Harry Brearley who at one stage worked for him, Kayser believed that 'a man's Vaterland was not the place where he is born, but the place where he is living and doing well'.

We were encouraged to speak 'educated Yorkshire', as it is sometimes known. The punishment of a thousand lines 'I must pronounce my aspirates', was sufficient incentive for most of us to at least try and speak a more acceptable dialect of Standard English. Perhaps it was this that separated us from our peers more than the bright red uniform, or indeed the curriculum. Equally, there was an opportunity to mix with young people of our own age from some of the more affluent areas of the City. Some had parents with cars. Some had even been abroad on holiday. Mostly they wore the Stewarts & Stewarts, or Cole Brothers brand of the school uniform and not the Co-op's which was the lot of the majority. Subtle differences in the styling were easily observed and the cheaper Co-op garb swiftly recognised as such. Despite these overt statements of class, there nevertheless existed a good atmosphere in the school and many long lasting friendships were made. The realisation, by the age of 16, that a better and more fulfilling life was to be had beyond the Wicker Arches was sufficient incentive, despite the attentions of a very attractive young lady, to pass a few 'O' levels.

Armed with a modest but adequate number of passes, the world of work beckoned. The prospect of higher education was not even a dream for most Grammar School students, especially those from a working class background. Our parents had 'kept' us for an extra year and that was as much as they felt able to do.

They worked and we were expected to join in, and quickly. The offer of a job at a local brewery was not greeted with enthusiasm by my parents, despite the family tradition of doing their best to bolster brewers' profits. In the late 1950s, in a time of full employment, failure to secure a job within a fortnight of leaving school was viewed not so much as being unfortunate, but as an adverse reflection on the individual's willingness to work.

My father was in steel; so was his father. I had uncles and cousins, all of whom had found their way into the clutches of Vulcan. In any case, I had been given the 'feel' for it and it was an industry with a vital role and an expanding future. In 1959 there were around 120 local companies engaged to a greater or lesser degree in the industry. Many of them were looking for trainees. From the outset my fate was sealed.

The local companies ranged in size from the giant English Steel Corporation, which employed over 13,000 people in its seven Sheffield works. They produced not only 500,000 tons of high grade steel per year, but were major manufacturers of a range of products as diverse as heavy castings and forgings to hacksaw blades and engineers tools. At the other extreme were the very small, highly specialised companies who perhaps employed less than a dozen. Being a very small cog in a very large wheel had few attractions and the offer of a job at a relatively small company, seemingly offered the best prospects.

Therefore, a sunny August morning saw me stepping off the No. 78 bus, knowing next to nothing of the company, what it produced or even what I would be doing. The Managing Director, whom I had met at the interview, had assured me that as a Commercial Trainee, I should not be put to making tea and that the position was worthy for such as had received our type of education (Firth Park and Repton). All this was uppermost in my mind as I walked down Wharf Lane, which had been the access to the wharves at the original terminus of the Sheffield and Rotherham Canal.

The Tinsley Rolling Mills Co Ltd was where I should earn my first £3 15s 0d a week, with a review after 3 months. Tinsley's history was similar to many of Sheffield's smaller steel companies and its eventual demise was typical.

Chapter Two

INDUSTRIAL REVOLUTION

HALLAMSHIRE'S MANUFACTURERS HAD long complained over the difficulties they experienced in shipping their wares out of the area. Long and tedious packhorse journeys had to be endured to reach the river ports of Blythe and Bawtry where their goods were transhipped, to eventually reach Stockwith, Gainsborough or one of the other major river ports of the time. Their main market was London, the extra carriage and handling necessarily increasing their costs. The canalisation of the River Don had begun in 1727 but it was not until 1751 that access to Tinsley was finally gained. It would be a further 68 years before the final stretch into Sheffield proper would be completed.

Upon completion of the canal, the Canal Company's original wharf and facilities at Tinsley became redundant and it was on this narrow spit of land, sandwiched between the river and canal, that in 1838 George Walter Dyson and Edward Wilkinson Shirt, decided they would site their new rolling mill. Locally, demand for rolled steel and iron products was rapidly growing and the site had several advantages. It offered ample water for cooling and steam generating purposes, good access to both road and water transport and most importantly it allowed coal to be barged directly to the works from the Tinsley Park Colliery. These significant advantages far out-weighed the spatial limitations of the 'island' site.

The canal as it is today, showing the original 'island' site of Tinsley Rolling Mills Co Ltd.

Mr Charles Cammell had arrived in Sheffield from Hull, to work as a travelling salesman for Ibbotson Brothers and he was able to guarantee sufficient work for the Tinsley mill to allow them to become well established. Cammell continued working for Ibbotson's until the opening of his own works on Savile Street in Sheffield. By 1851 Dyson & Shirt were advertising their services to the district's steel manufacturers with the announcement that they had erected:

'New and powerful steam machinery with all the latest improvements. Orders sent to the Company or the George Inn, bottom of High Street, Sheffield will be punctually attended to.'

The tradition of having a drink whilst doing business clearly goes back a long way! The Company had been officially constituted as Dyson, Shirt & Co in 1846 and when in 1874 Alderman George Neill joined them as Managing Director, the firm was reconstituted as The Tinsley Rolling Mills Co Ltd. Reorganisation followed again in 1897 when Charles Branson became Chairman and George Senior joined the Board of Directors. The first local Public Companies were John Brown & Co and Charles Cammell & Co who went public in 1864 and 1865 respectively. The cost and scale of mid-Victorian expansion was such that it could not be sustained by local finance for long. Stock market flotation allowed individuals to capitalise on their previous risk-taking and efforts. Some idea of the growth in local steelmaking may be judged by the 1835 production figure which was estimated to be in the order of 10,000 tons. Less than 30 years were to elapse before production was over 100,000 tons and rising.

Tinsley had from its earliest days concentrated on rolling, but 1877 saw them diversify with the installation of a 35 cwt steam hammer. With this they were able to produce compound or composite iron and steel bars for the production of edge tools and large knife blades. An edge tool fabricated entirely from tool steel is an expensive and unnecessary practice since the bulk of the blade is not required to keep a cutting edge. Combining the small requirement for tool steel on the cutting edge with the much larger and cheaper, iron backing material meant that substantial savings could be made. To quote from a contemporary document:

'Composite iron and steel provides the hardness where it is required and workability for drilling and shaping in the backup material'

The 35 cwt hammer would see considerable service, finally being scrapped in May 1950 when the existing work was transferred to C Meadows & Co Ltd. Very few of Tinsley's men were willing to be transferred to 'Cutty' Meadows as the works were commonly known, and they were offered work in other departments of the Tinsley works.

Tinsley's original offices with stacks of Bull Head Rail for re-rolling. This same building was formerly the terminal offices of the Canal Company. Sheffield City Libraries

Tinsley began to specialise in the rolling of special sections and flat products. They quickly gained a reputation for spring steels and, more especially, for grooved machete flats which an expanding Empire, much of which was in the Tropics, needed. These essential tools were so designed as to allow plant juices to easily drain away from the knife's cutting edge and thus inhibit clogging. The company would continue rolling these sections until the end of its independent existence, often to the chagrin of the Production Staff who would have been happier making more profitable items!

By the turn of the century, Britain's pre-eminence as the world's largest steel producer was a matter of history. Germany had overtaken us. In Sheffield, small companies like Tinsley were still the rule though there were notable exceptions, such as Cammells,

Vickers, Firths and Browns who could compete with anyone globally.

In 1904, Tinsley's Directors received a report from Slater Willis, the Company Secretary as to the Company's performance. This report gives a measure of the scale of working as well as a measure of the inefficiency of the industry.

Total sales of all products amounted to 4421 tons of which 34% went to the Managing Director's own company, James Neill & Co. In order to roll this tonnage, the re-heating furnaces consumed 6681 tons of coal and the Company employed 150 men. Each employee thus contributed just over 29 tons per year to production. By 1960 this figure was 150 tons! For each ton of steel rolled, 30 cwt of coal was needed. Annual profit was a 'very satisfactory' £2,748 7s 11d. Average sales prices were: Machete Sections: £8 12s 6d. per ton; Spring steels: £6 14s 7d. per ton. Raw material, mainly in the form of Bull Head rail crop ends cost £3 12s 6d per ton. Competition, it was reported, had been particularly severe during the year and some prices had been reduced by £2 0s 0d per ton on the prices charged four years earlier. The use of rail crops as raw material was carried on to a limited degree until the 1970s when, with the cessation of Bull Head rail production and more requirements for traceability of the source of the steel, the practice of slitting the rail into its 3 parts and then rolling them into flats ceased. Rails of course were manufactured from high grade carbon steel and were a perfectly acceptable alternative to using new steel billets.

The years between 1900 and 1902 saw the company diversify its products with the installation of a pair of sheet mills. These mills were restricted to a maximum width of 24 inches, which would eventually prove a liability for the tendency was for customers to demand even wider sheets, to cut down on waste. The mills were mainly introduced in order to meet a rising demand from the nation's rapidly developing agricultural engineering sector. The mills were driven by a Davy Brothers horizontal, tandem, compound steam engine which together with its coal fired boiler would be in use until 1951 when they were sold for scrap and replaced by a more modern electric drive. At the same time as the sheet mills were

Half Penny Bridge which crossed the Don, giving pedestrian access to the 'island' site of Dyson Shirt for a fee of ½d which was collected at the toll house. Sheffield City Libraries

introduced, the company built a shop for the manufacture of shovels and over the years this would become a major outlet for sheet production.

When Dyson & Shirt built their works, Tinsley was still a rural area, complete with its own picturesque cottages, barns and the famous 'Halfpenny' Bridge which crossed the Don. Blackburn Meadows were still 'sweet' enough to permit the playing of cricket by the works' team, and farm labourers toiled in the nearby fields. However, by the turn of the century, Tinsley was becoming increasingly industrialised as works were built along the Turnpike from both directions. Sheffield had only recently become a City and by 1900 it was already planning to acquire many of its smaller neighbours. Proposals to incorporate the Tinsley area were presented to Parliament in 1907 but the measure was met by strong opposition, not least from the local industrialists, who met '*to consider what steps should be taken to oppose the Sheffield Bill to incorporate Tinsley*'. Tinsley's Directors strongly supported opposition to the Bill despite their individual tendencies toward public service. George Neill had

The bridge spanning the River Don which started life as an over head crane, and to this day still spans the river.

served as Rotherham's Mayor on no less than five occasions and George Clarke, was Lord Mayor of Sheffield in 1901. The Bill was postponed, but the opposition was eventually overcome and by 1918 the whole Parish was absorbed into the City. Tinsley Rolling Mills had one other Director who would become Sheffield's Lord Mayor, Colonel Branson, who occupied the position at the outbreak of the First World War. The position of Master Cutler was one which Tinsley's Directors filled on no less than seven occasions, the last being Gilbert Willis in 1968/69.

The last year of peace before the First World War saw the Company's turnover reach £44,416 with profits totalling £3,905. By then, the limitations of the island site were obvious, with consequent restrictions on efficiency and profits. Company Secretary, Slater Willis gave the Board Meeting held on 23 March 1914, a summary of the options available. They were:

> To modernise on the existing site, but still be faced with physical limits to production. The site was a difficult one, being narrow and

virtually surrounded with water it would always limit what could be produced.

Alternatively, they could 'strike out' and cross the river and build 'the nucleus of a really modern works'.

He anticipated that the benefits, including having their own railway siding would, even after building a bridge to cross the river, be a saving of £125 a year and that with an anticipated increase in production, their ability to buy coal at a cheaper rate and to save carting to a rail(head) would save £3,000-£4,000 per year. An expected growth in the Company of 30-40% was expected.

'The new mill for quantity, the old mill for quality' became the slogan. The Board agreed that the second, expansionary option was the correct one and enquiries were initiated to acquire land from The South Yorkshire Canal Company and The Great Central Railway, who between them owned the site the Company sought.

Any plans for the immediate development of the new works were put into abeyance with the outbreak of war in August 1914. The initial reaction of the Company was to carry on as usual but with men flocking to join the forces, the Board was asked for a decision about paying the dependents of these men. At the time, the Company had only one reservist, a William Hough, but he had been joined by many of his workmates in the first flush of enthusiasm.

Much of what Sheffield produced in its steel and engineering works had a military value and the war created an insatiable appetite for everything that could be produced by Vulcan's devotees. Vickers increased their output of large guns from 300 to over 3,000 annually. Cammells and Firths were responsible for over a million shells each. Steel Peech and Tozer built an entirely new works as did Cammells. Tinsley carried on with increased effort and much longer hours. Profits reflected some of this and New Year's Day 1917 saw the Company becoming a Controlled Establishment under *The Munitions of War Act* of 1915 much to the concern of its Directors, who looked for assurances about the tax position. As wholesale carnage took place on the Battlefields, they were assured that they would still receive 20% of their standard profit even allowing for increased output. Business is after all about profit and it has been argued that the root cause of the First World War was commercial domination, rivalry and ultimately, profits.

The works were asked in 1916 to consider joining a local consortium to roll 20 gauge bullet proof sheet for the army who were demanding 1 million 'tin' helmets'...in a hurry. The specified material was 11/14% manganese which had initially been developed

Dixons of Sheffield pictured above, were one of the biggest producers of 'tin' helmets. Tinsley were asked to join a local consortium to roll 20 gauge bullet proof sheet for the army.

by Hadfields for its wear resisting properties. It was non-magnetic, tough and durable and Tinsley had no experience of working with it. It was however not expected to present any great problems and as supplies would be made available, calculations were made as to the joint effort needed to satisfy the Army. It would require $1\frac{1}{2}$ tons of rolled sheet to produce 1,000 helmet blanks and if the 20 mills in the area were to work day and night solely on the requirement, it would be 13 weeks before the whole order could be completed. But this was impractical; rolls would wear and need changing. These in turn would have to 'bed in' on easier work before rolling thin sheets. They concluded that a realistic forecast would be something in the order of 26 weeks. Sankeys in Bilston, it was known, could only press 30,000 helmet blanks a week'... so in any case they would need 33 weeks to complete the lot.

The helmets were completed, issued, used and would lay scattered among the ruined fields of Flanders later that year.

The Ministry of Munitions realised that without the full co-operation of all those engaged in the war effort at home, then the demands of the war machine could never be satisfied. As a consequence it was decided to give some recognition for their efforts. Sir Charles Stewart-Wilson, KGE duly wrote to the Company, along with many others, in November 1917 asking them to nominate 1% of the workforce for the award of the medal of the *Order of the British Empire* for outstanding merit. The Company replied (under the cover TOP SECRET) that as they only employed 150 people they would presumably only get one award but they felt both the Works Manager, John Marshall and the Head Roller, George Wainwright, both deserved the medal for their 'initiative, perseverance, and resource'. Being salaried, the Works Manager was quickly excluded by The Ministry. In acknowledging the decision, the Directors wrote saying they were not aggrieved since neither they nor the nominees had sought the award but pointed out most strongly that without John Marshall's enormous efforts the quantities of war materials the Company had supplied would never have been made. These included; shovels, helmet sheets, bullet proof sheets, spring steels, bars for aircraft magnetos, as well as components for gun cotton. In all this, the Works Manager's efforts had been crucial. There is no record of any official reply.

The war came abruptly to an end and in so doing the local steel industry was left facing a very uncertain future. Not so at Tinsley. The land for its expansion across the river had been acquired. The first, smaller plot cost £500 and the second larger area had been purchased from the Railway for £1,200. Both lots were in the Company's possession by the end of September 1916 and both had come within budget.

Plans went ahead rapidly and a steel framed and sheeted building was erected to house the mill and other ancillary equipment including a roll turning shop and an electric motor room. The immediate post-war years saw the boom quickly replaced by a serious economic downturn. In 1921 the local unemployment figure

A group of unemployed workers at a day centre in 1934.
Sheffield City Libraries

stood at 69,300 and not for the last time the City of Steel was a depressed area. The lessons the 1920s and 1930s provided, of not having a diverse local economy, would not be learned by later generations.

Tinsley though fared somewhat better than most. The decision to build a 12 inch double duo mill with variable drive designed specifically to meet the demands of the growing automotive industry was a wise one. Unlike the older industrial areas, parts of the country enjoyed an unrivalled prosperity and car ownership became a reality for many, with the consequence that the new mill was kept busy. As the Directors reported, '*The new mill is keeping the Company busy when many similar companies are facing hard times*'. The threat of renewed hostilities with Germany saw Sheffield and its neighbours again receiving demands for its warlike products, as re-armament got under way. This period of the late 1930s brought much needed economic relief to many hard pressed local companies. By 1938 so swift had been the growth in demand that some companies were even struggling to obtain steel to meet orders and the Admiralty were ordering armour plate from Czechoslovakia.

Tinsley were encouraged to extend the 12 inch mill building to cover a part of the Stockyard, to enable night shift working whilst complying with the likely blackout regulations. Orders for munitions work included; special components for aircraft gun turrets, bayonet blanks, rocket launcher rails plus the many profiles needed for lorries, cars and now tanks and bren gun carriers.

Declaration of war and the rapid mobilisation of the population created a problem which the Company had not experienced in the earlier hostilities. So effective was the 'call up' that despite the priority of much of its work, the mills were soon short of experienced labour and production suffered. Incredibly, in 1942 the Company faced a real prospect of closure. The shortage of men had seen them frequently only able to work 'short time' and this was reducing output to such an extent that revenue was insufficient to meet expenditure. In March they were overdrawn to the extent of £19,486 19s 2d. and with the arrival of a tax demand for £5,000 the Directors reluctantly called in an interest free loan of £3,000 they had earlier made to the Government. At this time, the Shovel

The ubiquitous Bren Gun carrier, which served on all fronts during World War Two. The construction was primarily from welded panels of bullet proof steel plate.

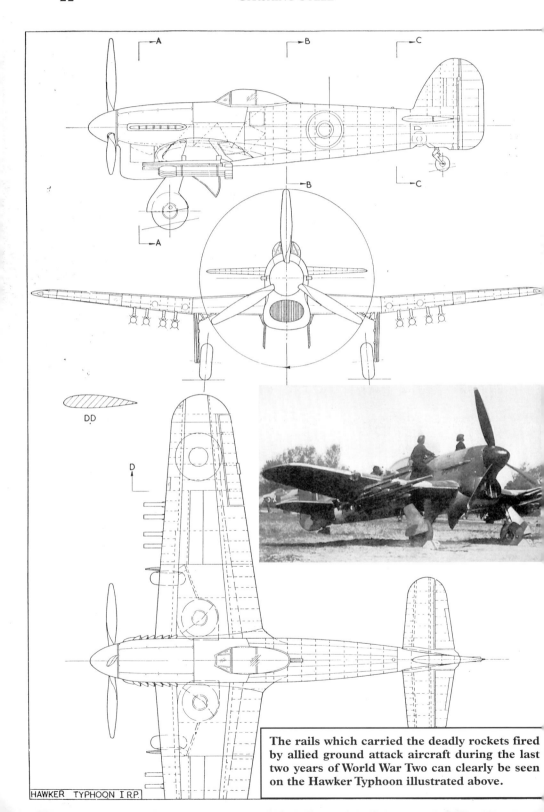

The rails which carried the deadly rockets fired by allied ground attack aircraft during the last two years of World War Two can clearly be seen on the Hawker Typhoon illustrated above.

HAWKER   TYPHOON I R.P.

Components for the gun turret of the Bristol Blenheim medium bomber, were manufactured in Sheffield from steel rolled at Tinsley Rolling Mills Co Ltd.

Department closed owing to the Company's inability to recruit suitable labour. It was fated never to re-open!

Sheffield's contribution to the country's War effort was immense. Despite air raids which affected nearly 80,000 households, the great industrial arsenal the City had become, continued producing its military wares. The foundries cast gun turrets, shell and bomb casings, including the 10 ton 'Grand Slam', which was the most destructive, non-nuclear, bomb ever made. The forges and machine shops churned out gun barrels, shells, aircraft components and crank shafts of all types including almost all of those for the Rolls Royce Merlin engine, which powered so many Allied aircraft during the Second World War. The rolling mills made armour plate for tanks, landing craft and battleships as well as many very mundane but essential products.

Metallurgical Research and Development ensured that alternatives were available for many of the highly alloyed steels in use, thereby saving on shipping space. New steels were developed for armour piercing shells, aircraft engines and armour plate.

Night and day the City toiled. Such was the ethic built upon the knowledge of their own excellence and recognition of the national

plight that there were few industrial disputes. The introduction
though of women into the works, did bring about a measure of
resentment over the role of these 'dilutees'. Dressed in their blue
overalls and colourfully contrasting 'turbans', they were to become a
familiar feature of post war Sheffield for unlike their mothers, many
of them were unwilling to return to 'domesticity'. Their contribution
to the City's war-time achievements was outstanding, as crane
drivers, inspectors, machinists, grinders, die-casters and a whole host
of other jobs which helped ensure that the armed forces received
their vital supplies.

In less than four decades, this supreme effort and sacrifice would
be forgotten by the cold Politico-Economists, who then governed the
Nation that had stood alone to defend Democracy.

Chapter Three

FORGING AHEAD

THE WAR'S ENDING NOT ONLY brought about universal relief but also a feeling that the depression which had so swiftly followed the Armistice of 1918 should never be repeated. The recently elected government led by Clement Attlee had received an overwhelming mandate to carry out wholesale changes in many of the nation's institutions which had been deemed, in the past, to have created an unjust society. Economically, the country was spent. The exertions of six years of total war had left the nation exhausted in all senses. A long period of austerity and consumer restraint was in store for a people who were desperate to loosen some of the shackles which, during total war they had accepted, perhaps not always willingly but certainly with an appreciation of their fairness.

Nationally, the steel industry had to come to terms with the changeover from a virtual command economy, to one where the consumer would dictate demand. Perhaps, in retrospect, it was an asset that the nation had such limited financial resources and that they were unable to find the foreign exchange needed to import the things which its population now craved. As it was, the nation was effectively bankrupt, and would only get itself out of this situation by earning foreign exchange. Britain's tired steel plants and its workers had some advantage though. They were intact. Most of our competitors' factories lay in ruin and only the fear of the spread of Communism from our erstwhile Soviet Allies would induce our other, richer American allies, who had prospered beyond measure from their involvement in the war, to attempt to halt its spread by aiding the rebuilding of Europe's industries with the implementation of the so called Marshall Plan. This would have ominous implications for the long-term prospects of Sheffield and its staple trade.

In 1946, total steel production nationally amounted to 12.9 million tons. Shortages existed for very many products both domestic and industrial. With only a limited amount of foreign exchange available, the importation of steel was controlled by the British Iron and Steel Corporation, who allocated it to the users. Tinsley was a recipient of a quantity of billets, originating in Japan, which were of such dubious quality that 10 years later, when I joined the Company, the billets were still lying, unloved, in a corner of the stockyard. The British Iron & Steel Federation had been requested

The modernised sheet mills. Tinsley Rolling
Mills Co. Ltd, c1960. Sheffield City Archives

to report on the modernisation of the Steel Industry by the wartime Coalition Government and they eventually reported that a programme costing £168 million would be needed to enable the complete modernisation of the industry. Meanwhile a question mark would hang over steel, with the Government's Manifesto pledge to bring the industry into public ownership remaining unfulfilled.

During the immediate post-war period and not for the last time, industry was exhorted to export. As a response, the Hon. Robert Balfour, who was also a Director of Tinsley, visited the USA and inspected a number of their steel plants. He reported to the Board on his return that:

> *'... whilst American sheet quality was better, it was not so much a matter of the mills themselves but more of the ancillary equipment with which they were equipped and also of the higher quality standards to which they worked'.*

A decision was made to modernise the sheet mills. The steam engine would be replaced by electric drive and the old coal fired re-heating furnaces would be replaced with more modern ones. Coal-fired furnaces were notoriously difficult to regulate, were prone to decarburise the steel, and were potentially very dirty, as the Company knew only too well. Oil, it was thought, was insecure, and as it had to be imported would not help the economy. Town gas was very controllable but would there be sufficient supply? Having received assurances that supply would not present any problems, the Company opted to install gas-fired furnaces and orders were placed with G P Wincott of Sheffield in March 1951. At the same time, orders were also placed with English Electric for the motor and with The Turbine Gear Co, for the drive and reduction gear.

The development was completed in 1953 but, as the Directors looked to the future of the sheet department with some optimism, they were quickly deflated with the news that James Neill & Co, who hitherto had been a major customer of the sheet mills, had just acquired their own mills by their takeover of The Hallamshire Steel & File Co. Despite this initial blow, the Directors were still confident that the modernisation placed them in a position to produce as good a sheet in finish and quality as anyone. Unfortunately their position in the market would be further undermined with developments which were taking place in Rotherham. Less than four years later, Steel Peech and Tozer would open a medium width continuous strip mill at Brinsworth. This mill, built at a cost of £6.5 million, had a capacity of 250,000-300,000 tons per year and sounded the death knell to all the old hand mills in the area except those which specialised in the production of the more highly alloyed steels. Tinsley had forsaken the rolling of sophisticated steels, mainly on account of their lack of a heat treatment plant, concentrating instead on qualities which where easier to produce. The modernised mill would continue working in an ever-diminishing market until closure in 1966, to make way for another bar mill.

The threat of Nationalisation had been lifted by 1952 and the case for completing the modernisation of the old works could not be ignored. The old, inefficient and smoke-polluting mills, it was hoped, could be replaced with financial assistance from the American Revolving Fund for Industry. A visit from a representative of The Board of Trade left the Directors feeling that a loan of £30,000 would be available. Consequently, tenders were issued in April 1953 for a new mill designed to replace the existing steam driven 8$^1/_2$″, 10$^1/_2$″ and 12$^1/_2$″ mills. An order was placed in the September with Brightside Foundry & Engineering for the supply of a 5 stand, 3 high 10 inch mill, complete with electrics, reduction gear, rolls, automatic lubrication and bed plate for an inclusive price of £23,222. Delivery would take 12-14 months but the electric motor would be a further 7 months!

Any expectations of financial assistance were dashed in February 1954 when the company were informed that despite earlier encouragement the scheme did not qualify and no help was available from the Fund. No doubt feeling aggrieved that German industry was being revived with the latest technology by American aid whilst we were being denied, they nonetheless decided to press ahead. Certainly, Gilbert Willis who by now had joined his father Slater, on the Board, felt that they should finance the development themselves.

He produced the following simple figures:

Liquid Assets (excluding stock and investments):	£71,950
Cost of new plant and building:	£64,700
Excess of assets over new plant:	£7,250
Estimated increase in stock to supply new mill:	£24,000
Overdraft required:	£16,750

Gilbert Willis agreed to a suggestion that he should go along to the Company's bankers on George Street and see what they would do. In any case, it was noted no-one had seen the Bank Manager for a year! Without a Business Plan in triplicate, he would, no doubt, have been laughed out nowadays, but the banking system then was perhaps more in tune with local needs than it is currently, and in any case the Company had integrity and was run by 'gentlemen'. The outcome of the meeting was an offer of an overdraft of £50,000, if it

Tinsley Rolling Mills Co, Ltd. New 10 inch mill showing differing floor levels, chutes and conveyors, c1960. Sheffield City Archives

were needed. No doubt the Bank Manager felt the Company had under-estimated. The old debate about which fuel to use in the re-heating furnace was again aired. Experience with the modern stoker fed 12 inch mill furnace showed that coal would cost 8s 6d. per ton of steel rolled. The gas-fired sheet mill furnaces were expensive to operate, costing 18s 6d per ton and estimates for using oil indicated a figure of 12s 6d per ton. Coal was secure, gas was now too expensive and oil was still viewed with some suspicion, relying as it did on imports. The decision was made to go for coal with the design being suitable for easy conversion to alternative fuels should they become more competitive in the future. Finally, an order was placed for the mill building. Physical constraints, it was hoped, could be minimised by experimenting with floor levels, underfloor chutes and conveyors. These, it was firmly expected, would not only economise on space, but make the physical strain on the mill team somewhat easier.

The Company Annual General Meeting in June 1955 heard a report on the opening of the new mill and the Directors were also able to report

> *'the final closure of 7 old, smoke producing furnaces during the past 2 years with the result of a much cleaner atmosphere and better working conditions'.*

No doubt the Council's smoke abatement officer was also very pleased. The large notice at the entrance to the works imploring employees to take all steps to minimise smoke emissions, was removed. The only smoke now invading the works was to come from the Power Station across the railway line.

The final stage of the modernisation plan was the building of two amenity blocks complete with showers and special facilities for the increasing numbers of Muslims then being employed.

Steel production within the UK had risen to 24.7 million ingot tons by 1959. Exports of steel were running at an annual rate of nearly 3 million tons, which was a higher figure than the USA or Japan. Government exhortation had been listened to and the industry was buoyant and in an expansionist mood.

Some indication of this mood, locally, may be gauged by the extent of a number of recent developments.

Edgar Allen & Co Ltd
1953-1959: £1,240,000 in general works development.

Arthur Balfour & Co Ltd
1958: A new high frequency melting unit of 2 furnaces became operational. 3:10 ton gas fired heat treatment furnaces installed.

Darwins Ltd
1960: Production facilities for magnets extended.

Darwins Bright Steels Ltd
A new wire works completed at a cost of £160,000. Capacity increased from 12 tons a week to 30 tons.

Beeley Wood Forge
3 ton hammer rebuilt, additional 5 cwt and 10 cwt hammers installed. New boiler installed.

Brown Bayley Steels Ltd
1956: 24 ton arc furnace installed. New cold strip mill installed both at a cost of £260,000. 10⅝ inch double duo mill installed.
1957: 2 new 45 ton open hearth furnaces came into production at a cost of £600,000.
1959: Updating of one open hearth furnace cost £185,000.
1960: Updating Manningham Road forge cost £700,000.

English Steel Corporation
1960: Plans for new Greenfield site, est. £26 million due to open.
1963: Additional melting capacity at River Don Works.

Firth Brown
1959: New 800 ton forging press completed.
1960: New vacuum melting department cost £400,000.

Firth Vickers Stainless Steels Ltd
1957: Bar mills modernised. Additional 18 inch and 10 inch mills.
1958: A 12 inch cold rolling strip mill installed.
1960: Bar treatment plant extended and modernised.

Shepcote Lane Rolling Mills
1957/58: Hot rolling strip mills converted to STECKEL operation.
1959: Scheme to increase production from 450 to 800 tons a week announced.

Hadfields Ltd
1959: The 2,700 ton press completely overhauled. Conversion of coal fired boilers and plant to oil completed.

Arthur Lee & Sons Ltd
New works at Ecclesfield started operation.

Samuel Osborn & Co. Ltd
1957: New foundry on a 73-acre site at Halfway completed.

Sanderson Kayser Ltd, Newhall Road Works
1958: The 10 inch bar mill came into production.
1959: Grinding shop for machine knives re-equipped.

1960: A vacuum melting furnace installed.
1960: Second vacuum furnace installed. Improvements to billet heating and annealing furnaces.

Carlisle Street Works

1956: 10 inch double duo mill came into operation.
1958: New building and new annealing furnaces.
1960: New laboratory and additional straightening equipment introduced.

Steel Peech & Tozer Ltd

Capital expenditure since 1945: £32 million.
1957: A continuous hot strip mill commissioned cost £6.5 million.
1959: Vacuum casting plant commissioned.
1960: The semi-continuous bar mill modernised at a cost of £400,000.
Plans well underway to convert Templeborough melting shop into an all-electric operation.

Samuel Fox & Co Ltd

Capital expenditure since 1945: £24 million.
1954: New stockyard and 70 ton electric furnace - £2 million
1957: At a cost of £3 1/2 million a second and larger electric furnace commissioned. Modernisation of billet mill begun.
1958: Combined rod and bar mill installed at a cost of £3 million
New laboratory built.
1959: Work begun on a new hot mill for stainless sheet and light plate - capacity 11,000 tons per annum.

These were not actions that the City's hard-headed steel bosses would contemplate had they not been supremely confident about the future of the industry and its role in the nation's economic life. Order books were full as were wage packets. This was a period of full employment, proof indeed that the unwritten national aim was for the Government to manage the economy so as to maintain full employment and all political parties had reached a consensus over this objective.

The Conservative Manifesto for that year's Election summed up the widely felt position:

'The British economy is sounder today than at any time since the First World War. Sterling has been re-established as a strong and respected currency... Our exports have reached the highest peak ever.'

These were the days of Harold Macmillan's *'You've never had it so good'*. The generation born during the war years were the first to enjoy universal education, health and rock and roll. The future looked set fair with more, many more, increases in living standards as a result of full employment.

Chapter 4

STARTING OUT

M Y INITIATION INTO THE DUOTHEISM of Vulcan and Mammon began that August morning, with the wind in the East and the aroma from the sewage works at Blackburn Meadows offending my nostrils. In order to reach the Company's far from imposing offices, the canal had to be crossed by way of an 18th Century brick bridge. This further added to the problems being suffered by my olfactory sense, since the canal, like the river, was a conduit for the waste, oily water draining from countless factories along its banks. Sheffield could lay claim to having some of the most polluted water systems in the Western world - visible proof of the old Yorkshire truth of 'where there's muck there's money'.

I was introduced to the twenty or so other members of staff and then shown around the works. Next it was in to see Mr Willis. In my naivety, I expected that the good-natured, almost amusing way in which he had interviewed me, would be repeated when I came to work with him and was somewhat taken aback by the stern, headmasterly, manner he was now exhibiting. I quickly realised that the nature of being an actual employee, was different from the courtship he had used in persuading me to join them. With the arrogance and ignorance of youth, I had really thought that he needed me and that I was the vital rejuvenating spark that would change the Company and, in gratitude, I should be at least made a local Director within months. Fifteen minutes later, armed with a list of jobs in the works, which I was told I was expected to 'have a go at', including tea mashing, I left his office chastened and just a little wiser.

A modern Safety Officer would no doubt be horrified, but with supervision I drove a crane, cut a billet, charged it into a furnace, pulled it out, white hot, and took it to the cogging stand. Eventually I even plucked up sufficient courage to feed a moving white-hot bar into the finishing stand. By the time I had finished my stay in the works' offices I had completed my list of duties. I had not only experienced, albeit briefly, the real work environment, but I also gained even more admiration and respect for those who endured it on a daily basis. I could estimate weights, use a crack detector, a

Brinell machine and I even knew a little about steel specifications. In the future I never missed an opportunity to get into the works ... often to the chagrin of my immediate boss who failed to understand my interest and personally kept out of the place as much as possible.

I had loathed mathematics whilst at school. Masters had despaired, not only of my apparent lack of ability, but more so about my very obvious lack of interest in the topic. Amazingly, as a commercial trainee, I spent most of my time calculating and learning to estimate steel prices. If ever there was just reason to suspect school teachers' abilities and judgement, I was proof of how wrong they could be. I was applying mathematics on a daily basis and enjoying it! Steel prices were largely determined by the Iron and Steel Board who issued schedules of maximum prices that could be charged for a large range of steel products. They arrived at their prices by gathering cost data from a whole range of steel producers to arrive at an average cost. The average company, if there ever was one, would then make an average profit. As it was, some items were profitable; others would lead to a loss. Knowledge of costs was therefore essential if mistakes were to be avoided.

Individual Steel Associations existed, each dealing with a product or a geographical area. These associations issued their own price lists, some of which dealt with products not covered by the Board's schedules. In all cases where two lists were published there would be, in effect, one price since the associations' prices would be minima but the same as the Board's which were maxima.

We were members of The Sheffield & District Rollers & Tilters Association and operated their prices for most sheet products and also for some bars where the Board's prices were too low for us. This Association bar price list was known as List 'A', but by some customers as the 'Gold Platers List', and with good reason. Mild steel was in this category, being a product locally widely despised as 'clog iron', and largely manufactured in the Black Country, where their mills were more suited to its production. When this mundane product was offered by almost all of Sheffield's mills, its high price was justified by a loophole in the Board's schedules which allowed mills which 'hand rolled to a special finish and/or fine tolerance in a mill designed for the production of High Speed and/or Tool Steels', to charge a premium. In times of steel shortages it could be a useful opportunity to maximise profit.

The SDRTA was something of a Gentlemen's Club, meeting monthly at The Royal Victoria Hotel. Very occasionally, as a very young man, I was deputed to attend the meeting as the Company's fifth reserve and despite some trepidation, always found the 'G and T' sufficient reward for the nerve-racking experience. Some of the men around the table had reputations which were far from complimentary; they were mean or untrustworthy but worst of all they broke agreements. Perhaps there may have been some truth in the stories, but I was always treated politely if I made a small contribution to the proceedings. The Association should not have discussed price fixing, but they did. Restrictive practices were not solely the responsibility of Trades Unions.

Working out a price was a repetitive and at times, deadly dull occupation. It required a knowledge of steel specifications and there were hundreds of them; British, American, German, French, Swedish and Japanese were the most common. If the details weren't available in our 'library', a phone call to Sheffield Central Library's excellent Technical Library would usually bear fruit. Daily and perhaps on hundreds of occasions, the routine would be carried out - what type of steel is it? which list to use? does it need a cost price building up? what is the base price? are there any restrictions on analysis which carry extras; what is the extra for size; what, if any, is the extra charge for cutting to a length? what is the quantity per

Typical steel specifications. (B.S 970, 1955 EN Series)

SILICON-MANGANESE SPRING STEEL
BARS FOR OIL HARDENING AND TEMPERING

Chemical composition. The steel shall contain :

Element	En 45		En 45A	
	Per cent		Per cent	
	min.	max.	min.	max.
Carbon	0·50	0·60	0·55	0·65
Silicon	1·50	2·00	1·70	2·00
Manganese	0·70	1·00	0·70	1·00
Sulphur	—	0·050	—	0·050
Phosphorus	—	0·050	—	0·050

Dimensions. Laminated spring plates to this specification shall conform to the dimensional requirements in Appendix C. Steel of this type may also be required in the form of wire for oil-hardened and tempered springs (see B.S. 1429, ' Annealed steel wire for oil-hardened and tempered springs ').

1 PER CENT CHROMIUM-VANADIUM SPRING STEEL
BARS FOR OIL HARDENING AND TEMPERING

Chemical composition. The steel shall contain :

Element	Per cent	
	min.	max.
Carbon	0·45	0·55
Silicon	—	0·50
Manganese	0·50	0·80
Chromium	0·80	1·20
Vanadium	0·15	—
Sulphur	—	0·050
Phosphorus	—	0·050

Dimensions. Laminated spring plates to this specification shall conform to the dimensional requirements in Appendix C. Steel of this type may also be required in the form of wire for oil-hardened and tempered springs (see B.S. 1429, ' Annealed steel wire for oil-hardened and tempered springs ').

En 46

SILICON-MANGANESE SPRING STEEL
BARS FOR WATER HARDENING AND TEMPERING

Chemical composition. The steel shall contain :

Element	Per cent	
	min.	max.
Carbon	0·35	0·45
Silicon	1·50	2·00
Manganese	0·70	1·00
Sulphur	—	0·050
Phosphorus	—	0·050

Dimensions. Laminated spring plates to this specification shall conform to the dimensional requirements in Appendix C.

1 PER CENT CHROMIUM SPRING STEEL
BARS FOR OIL HARDENING AND TEMPERING

En 4

Chemical composition. The steel shall contain :

Element	Per cent	
	min.	max.
Carbon	0·45	0·55
Silicon	0·10	0·50
Manganese	0·50	0·80
Chromium	1·00	1·40
Sulphur	—	0·050
Phosphorus	—	0·050

Dimensions. Laminated spring plates to this specification shall conform to the dimensional requirements in Appendix C.

delivery, does it carry an extra? is there an extra zonal delivery charge? The whole process had to be carried out accurately and there were no pocket calculators to ease the burden. Each price was then checked. No amount of checking will ever be totally foolproof; the human factor will always slip through in any system. The worst scenario for the Sales Office was to have the costing department show up a loss caused by a price error. Fortunately they were very rare, but the inevitable 'dressing down' that such an event invoked was always incentive enough to redouble the dreaded checking. It was good training though, as was my introduction to the complications of export, and shipping documentation, which I was later to find I had a flair for. This proved to be a pleasing discovery to my immediate boss, who had always found it a chore and gladly passed it over to me.

A series of visits to other companies' works was organised for me, no doubt to widen my experience. Forges, foundries, melting shops, billet mills and heat treatment plants were all on my itinerary. Each had its own impact on the senses which, initially, could quickly

Molten steel being tapped from a Kaldo Unit into a ladle at Park Gate Iron and Steel Co. Ltd, Rotherham.

Tinsley Rolling Mills Co. Ltd. 12″ mill c.1960. In the background can be seen the actual rolling mill with finished bars and the shear driving gear in the foreground (Sheffield City Archives)

become disoriented by the combined effects of noise, heat and sometimes smell. Electric arc steelmaking could be an awesome experience. The noise generated by many thousands of volts of electricity as they made contact via the graphite electrodes with the scrap charge was quite simply terrifying. A deep sense of insecurity and foreboding was the strongest emotion to be experienced as the rumblings, loud clangings and muffled explosions reached a very loud crescendo. Tapping a furnace was a visual extravaganza, in my case usually viewed at a safe distance, unlike the furnace operatives who in their protective wear tended the monster with equanimity. Drop forges and stamps offered a variation on the visual and aural experiences on offer. Apart from the loud noise of metal making contact with metal under considerable force, flying millscale is an ever present danger, as is the possibility of the white hot work piece bursting with potentially lethal results. Rolling mills though represent man's continuous control over his work, and whilst there are ever present dangers, perhaps my familiarity with rolling made me feel less insecure. Grinding could be noisy, but the main reaction as with most engineering shops, was the peculiarly pleasant and ever present smell of soluble oil, which lingers on the clothes.

Tinsley's 12 inch mill, was known variously as 17 or 3 Dept. The entrance to the mill was by way of a door adjacent to the amenity block, with its ever present aromas of hand cleanser and sweat. Immediately to the left of the entrance were the large bar shears which made a very distinctive 'clank' as the shear blade made contact with the steel being cut. An experienced ear could tell by the sound, whether they were cutting hard or soft material. Enquiries would quickly be made if the sound was an unexpected one, stringent measures had long been in place to minimise the chances of a rogue billet of steel being rolled, but it sometimes happened and detection at the shears was better than a roasting from the customer. A little further on, to the right, was the motor room which housed the 500hp electric motor, the control gear and, most imposingly, the large flywheel. Old hands joked that if it were ever to break lose it would end up in Attercliffe! Fortunately it never did! The load the motor was taking was recorded on a moving chart which was the subject of a daily efficiency report to the Managing Director, Mr Willis. All mill stoppages had to be accounted for to him and reasons supplied. 'Down time' for whatever reasons had the Works Engineer or the Works Director summoned to his office for explanations. The Managing Director at Rotherham Forge was even rumoured to have a gauge fitted under his desk and the unscheduled sight of a stationary needle would result in a phone call from him demanding to know why the mill was standing idle. Time, after all, is money and the breed of hands-on managers in the Sheffield District, knew this only too well.

The rolling mill itself consisted of pairs of solid, cast steel housings; between each were two pairs of chilled iron or cast steel rolls which were coupled to the next set by cast iron pinions and boxes. The theory of using cast iron for the coupling was that being fairly brittle, they would, in the event, break before a more expensive roll would fracture - with potentially dangerous results. Wooden 'fillers' were sometimes strapped to the pinions so as to keep the boxes in position. When working at some speed, a rolling mill makes a quite distinctive 'clank, clank', as loose boxes and pinions meet together. This sound was accompanied by the 'flap, flap' of a hot bar running along the cast iron floor plates which covered the working area. To this cacophony there was added the sound of a crane whirring overhead as it moved billets or bars around the shop.

When a hand operated rolling mill was working well, there was a definite sense of purpose and rhythm. This manifested itself in the seemingly effortless way the mill team handled the hot steel. The rolling process began with the furnaceman, who often could gauge

24" Plate mill at Rotherham Forge and Rolling Mills Co. Ltd.

temperature by sight as effectively as any instrument. Armed only with a pair of long tongs he would drag the billets out of the furnace one at a time, once they had reached rolling temperature (1000/1100°C) and place them on a trolley which would be pushed across the cast iron floor, then put in a position for the cogger to push them into the cogging rolls. The showers of hot scale which had been removed as a result of the rolls' pressure on the billet rapidly accumulated on the floor and had to be regularly removed by a mill hand. The billet then progressed through the sucessive stands, each time being handled by a different mill operative.

The sets of rolls had a different series of profiles or 'plugs' machined into them. The skill of the roll designer was to ensure that the finished bar was neither under or over size, after due allowance was made for contraction when cooling. As the bar progressed along the line it became smaller, longer and its speed through the rolls would increase proportionately. Finally, the Roller himself would guide it into the finishing stand from where it would pass down a series of driven rollers to the cooling pit. Maybe 60 feet long travelling at up to 30 mph, the whip of a bar as it passed through a mill stand could be fearsome. A pile of disused cast iron boxes or a metal post strategically placed would give the operative a measure of protection, but his safety was his own experience telling him, almost instinctively, where to place his steel toe-capped feet and when to side step. Like most things in a steel works, constant observation and awareness were of the utmost importance if disaster was to be avoided. Like the coal industry which reckoned on the spirit and trust exhibited underground by the miners to maintain safety. Equally, the mill workers could only function by skilled teamwork

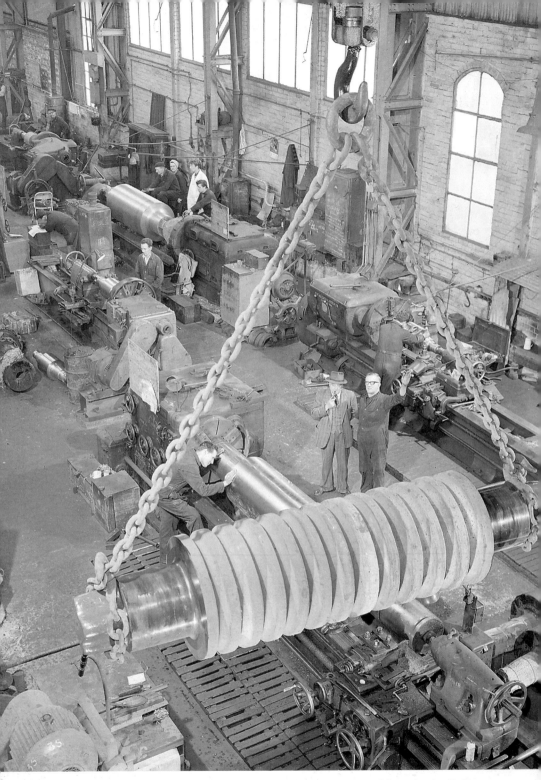

Preparing rolls in a roll shop. Among the group of four at the Lathe in the middle background is a woman wearing a 'turban', which indicates that the photograph was taken during, or soon after World War Two.

and being able to rely on their fellows. A good team was an important asset to a Company - a poor one a liability. The skills built up over years and passed on were as vital to a profitable operation as good management or equipment. Strangely though, they never appeared in a Balance Sheet as an asset! Labour could be disposed of easier than bricks and mortar as later events would show.

Dyson and Shirts original works was reached by crossing Slater Willis' 1920s river bridge. This consisted of an old, very substantial, overhead crane which had been obtained as a cheaper and quicker alternative to buying a purpose-built bridge. And, after modification, had proved a very satisfactory alternative. You then passed the office block, of which little can be said, except it was really quite unsuitable for a business which had expanded and now employed far more staff than the building could sensibly house. Expansion of the office space was not a high priority to this production-oriented company. The old site, which had been modernised by 1955, contained various relics of an earlier time. The stables, now used as a store and garage, were still intact. This was the Storeman's domain and nothing was ever issued from there without a stores' chit. As an old regular army man, of which we had many, Ben the storeman could always be relied on for a good tale as was another character called 'Dido' who had served in Russia in 1919 and gave graphic descriptions of how the British Army had helped the 'Whites' and hindered the 'Reds'.

The sheet mills, seldom had sufficient work for them both to be used at the same time. The quality was excellent, finish superb but with such low output these obsolescent mills struggled to make

An automatic cooling bed designed to assist the bars to cool evenly, thus maintaining their straightness.

money. The new mill, Steel Peech & Tozer had commissioned at Brinsworth was taking so much of Tinsley's business, that it was only a matter of time before the inevitable occurred. Until then, the old Tinsley sheet mill continued to roll on. Sheet and thin plate was mainly supplied to the agricultural engineering companies of which at the time Sheffield had many.

A decision was eventually taken, and in 1966 the sheet mills were replaced with a very modern 8 inch mill of radical design, utilising sleeves rather than solid rolls. Roll changing was made much easier and, as a consequence, less costly in 'down' time. Another innovation, at least as far as Tinsley was concerned, was that it employed a system of 'repeaters'. These guides made savings in manpower and therefore costs. At the time of its installation this mill was state of the art, and as such was blessed with its share of teething problems, many of which were solved but others niggled on throughout its working life. When it was first delivered to the works, the mill housings had been wrapped in a protective film and with the spindle shafts protruding at an angle they looked like replicas of the then very popular Daleks, of BBC's *Dr Who* fame. They were instantly christened as such and the mill was known from then on as the Dalek Mill.

There were a number of special sections which Tinsley had rolled for perhaps a century or more. These traditional lines had helped make the Company's reputation and despite the small quantities ordered, they were classic examples of mills taking 'the rough with the smooth'. They were the bane of the Manager Ken McKenzie's life. If too many 'sickle', 'hook', 'rat trap flats' or 'machete blades' were planned in a week, then production figures would look sick, bonuses deflated and his look of disgust increased in proportion to the low tonnage rolled.

The Managing Director was Lieutenant Colonel Gilbert Slater Willis, 'Sir' or 'GSW' were his accepted forms of address, but everyone knew him as Gilbert. Together with the Works Director, Colonel John Neale, usually referred to as 'Big John', they ran the Company, and as befitted their background, with absolute military order. No-one ever seemed to walk as they went about their duties, they more or less marched. Everyone worked strictly to orders, authority was delegated within clearly defined limits and whilst initiative wasn't totally discouraged, it was best to get the seal of approval from on high before putting any new idea into practice!

The Company had many loyal, long-serving employees and excellent relations with the local Unions. The British Iron, Steel &

Kindred Trades Association branch always invited the Directors and Staff to their annual dinner, where one of the Directors was expected to address the members with a few encouraging words about the future of the Company. Gilbert would be seen at some part of each day, clad in his old raincoat and Trilby hat, prowling round the works - a word of encouragement here, a question there. All helped keep good the relationships within the works. Perhaps the knowledge that he had on occasion used his influence to 'prod' the system on an employee's behalf, softened his seemingly cold manner making him a more human and respected individual.

The Sales Offices of steel companies did little actual selling, simply responding to the enquiries they received, with a price and a delivery date. Orders were obtained not so much on price, which were generally the same from all the companies, but more on reliability and service. Of course there was competition and a need to expand the Company's customer base, but this expansion was usually achieved by offering a quicker delivery than normal. New customers were often retained if delivery promises were kept and they had no cause to complain over quality. The early 1960s saw steel being at times, unofficially rationed with deliveries extending over many months. The offer of delivery within 2/3 weeks was frequently sufficient incentive to gain a new customer.

All of this was very cosy: the absence of real competition encouraged complacency and with it, inefficiency. Not that the industry was any worse than it had ever been, but much of it used old technology and managements were often still in the mould of Sheffield's 'Little Mesters'. They were myopic, easily satisfied and, despite increasing levels of investment, were unwilling or unable to think the unthinkable. Recognition that there were too many small units operating without any of the economies of scale came very late in the day and with dire consequences.

Chapter 5

AMALGAMATION AND MODERNISTATION

UNITED STEELS WAS CREATED IN 1917, with the merging of several companies as a result of the production demands of the First World War. The slump years which followed the war's end resulted in the creation of two other huge local concerns - English Steel Corporation (which merged the interests of Cammels and Vickers) and Thomas Firth and John Brown Limited. In contrast, the immediate post Second World War years saw uncertainty over nationalisation followed by a period of independent modernisation rather than of acquisitions and mergers. By the 1960s there were signs that the logic of companies merging their interests would not only bring cost benefits, but product range diversification would make the companies better able to compete. Sir Stuart Goodwin had already created the Neepsend Steel & Tool Corporation which consisted of a conglomeration of small companies operating with an apparent degree of autonomy. Being part of a 'group', created not only a diversity of products with a diminished risk in a recession, but also with a combined 'group', access to greater capital and bank borrowing.

In 1960 the very old and well established company of Sanderson Brothers and Newbould merged with Kayser (of The Brushes!) Ellison, to create Sanderson Kayser Limited. The new firm had a range which included; electrically melted special steels, machine knives, saws and engineering products. The company employed over 1,700 people at their various works around the city.

1961 saw Arthur Balfour & Company Limited merge with Darwins Limited to form Balfour Darwins. Again, a wide range of steel products came under the umbrella of one organisation as did a multiplicity of sites. Balfours employed 1,450 at their Capital Steel Works in The Wicker and Greenland Road sites. The latter was a fairly modern plant but included C Meadow's old canal side premises. Darwins employed 2,300 at six sites around the city. True integration, with its more efficient use of resources was a problem that could only be solved by a massive and costly programme of concentrating activities, logically, upon one site - a problem which for any of the emerging groups would require an investment programme of enormous proportions. The market supremacy which had created the giant Vickers, Cammels, Firths and Browns was no longer at Sheffield's disposal, nor were there the local entrepreneurs, for like the wealth the industry had produced, they too had left the City. Sheffield may still have been the industrial capital of Yorkshire, but finance and commerce were to be found elsewhere, and not necessarily in the region.

There is currently a widely held view that Sheffield just produced crude steel, but this is incorrect. Much of what was melted ended up being utilised within the city to produce tools, saws and other engineering products. The same companies who melted, rolled and forged steel were frequently manufacturers of finished engineering goods as well. This form of integrated activity had been one of the City's strengths and it had been recognised as such. Sheffield was as much a steel consumer as a producer, while its pre-eminence in finding solutions to metallurgical problems was world renowned. The engineering Group of Vickers had ready access through their links with English Steel Corporation to this expertise, which was fully utilised in the fields of aerospace, nuclear power and defence. It was the small companies, of which there were many, who in the 1960s started to feel exposed, by their very size, to the prospects of Britain's membership of the EEC and the threat of something almost unheard of, real competition!

Tinsley had, as chairman, Lord Riverdale, who as a member of the Balfour family had recently merged their business with Darwin's. As a part of my training I was seconded to their offices in order to widen my knowledge of export practice. They were in the midst of much organisational change and the staffs of the two companies were still operating with different pay rates, hours and indeed mentalities. At the Wicker plant for example, Darwin's staff did not have to clock on whilst Balfour's did. Every working night an impatient queue of Balfour staff would form alongside the clocking machine just to get away. As a secondee I chose not to benefit from the 'clocking' experience. Nor did I initially stand to attention in the canteen whenever a Director came into the room, until it was pointed out to me that I was the only one to remain seated. *'When in Rome and all that.....'.* Balfours may have made excellent steel, but the reconstituted potato they served up was dire in the extreme, and probably accounted for the low cost of their canteen dinners.

Despite a 12 year modernisation programme there was little evidence of it at Capital Steelworks, its application having been concentrated at their Greenland Road works. Capital Steelworks was a survivor from a bygone era. New ideas did not appear to be encouraged, while office methods were neo Dickensian. Customers' orders were glued into large ledgers to ensure they were never mislaid. When I asked, *'What happens if a ledger goes astray?'* I was simply told, *'they never have'*. Like numerous similar companies, they were deep in a rut and seemingly didn't care: secure in their well-established trade worldwide, a trade which was profitable and by and large, their customers bought what they were offered. Seemingly it occurred to no-one to enquire if the customer desired something different.

From the earliest days of crucible steel melting, which relied upon experience in mixing an assortment of ferro-alloys in varying proportions to achieve a given property, the City's steel manufacturers had encouraged a mystique about all things steel related. In those early days, temperatures had to be judged by the operatives using skill and experience and observation of the crystals in a broken ingot was the sole means of assessing a steel's grade. By the turn of this century, analytical methods had been introduced and techniques perfected to reliably produce all manner of steel grades, without recourse to the traditional methods deriving entirely upon skill. Nonetheless, the tool steel manufacturers clung on to the tradition of giving their special steels brand names. Stories abounded as to why steels with identical analyses but manufactured by different firms, produced different results. Perhaps like beer it was in the water?

Balfours had a large range of steel qualities which they regularly produced and consequently a similar number of brand names. They actually had a Department whose sole responsibility was to ensure that every bar had the correct label varnished onto it. Labels in Chinese, Spanish, English and surprisingly even Russian, told the recipient typically;

> *'Forge at a temperature of 1000/1100oC. Heat slowly and soak well, the time of soaking depending on the size of the piece being forged. Do not forge below Cherry Red....750/800oC'*

Catalogues and handy guides to tool steel selection were produced and distributed by all the manufacturers and must have been good business for the local printers. 'Hand on Heart', AB75, ULTRA CAPITAL, INVINCIBLE and VIADUCT, were typical of the Victorian names given to the special tool steels although some of them were not so special, being of ordinary commercial quality which now benefited from a brand name and hence a much higher price! Turning sows ears into silk purses had long been a traditional

SAMUEL OSBORN
& CO., LIMITED
SHEFFIELD · ENGLAND
"TITAN"
MANGANESE STEEL
 MANG

 SAMUEL OSBORN
& CO., LIMITED
SHEFFIELD · ENGLAND
"TRIPLE MUSHET"
HIGH SPEED STEEL
(ANNEALED)
GZ6

Typical labels showing the mystique perpetuating names given to special steels. The manufacture of these labels alone provided excellent business for label and adhesive tape makers.

method for boosting profits. Harry Brearley mentions in his memoirs how Kayser had confided in him, that he had made most of his money out of old railway engine tyres. These were the high quality, hot forged, machined steel outer rims of a locomotive driving wheel. He graded them and, after rolling them into bars, sold them on as crucible tool steel!

Even those producers of general engineering alloy steels often used their 'experience' as a basis of their marketing. A 1954 piece of publicity from Wm Jessop typifies the approach; almost mystical in tone it reads:

> *'The essential data for a special steel may be condensed into a few words, figures and symbols. The true formula is made up of intangibles of skill, knowledge and testing aimed at the development and production of a special steel for a special purpose'*

Not only was mystique important to the local steel industry, it also seemed important for some firms, to continue using as much ancient plant as possible in the belief that it alone could be used for working the special steels being produced. Balfours had even claimed in their publicity that their current use of an ancient rope driven mill, worthy of exhibiting in the Science Museum, was justified on the grounds that it allowed more flexibility. Unfortunately our continental competitors were not impressed by this argument and were equipping their mills with modern highly efficient machinery.

There was also a tendency for customers to be shown a 'take it or leave it' attitude by many of the City's manufacturers. This attitude can still unfortunately, occasionally be observed in the approach to public relations by more than one of the biggest of the larger companies still operating in 'Steel City'.

Typically, a request from abroad for less than a cast quantity of a non-British steel specification would in the 1960s almost certainly be met by a flat refusal to supply, or the offer of a British Standard Steel near equivalent. All too frequently this negative attitude threw customers into the open arms of their competitors, who may also offer better delivery and terms of payment, as added inducement to move away from Sheffield steel.

Ominously, between 1960 and 1963, European Coal and Steel Community bulk steel production rose by 11 million tons, while consumption, only increased by $6^{1}/_{2}$ million tons - a warning signal for future profits. During this period several traditional Empire markets - Canada, India, Australia and South Africa - inaugurated production in their own steel industries and were able not only to satisfy their own demand, upon which we may have been too reliant in the past, but were able to export surpluses, some of which would be sold on the British market. However, the major threat was from Japan, which had embarked upon an expansionist industrial policy at the heart of which lay the staples of shipbuilding and steelmaking. Not only were they taking an increased share of Britain's traditional export markets, but they were also penetrating the British market and supplying significant quantities of high quality steels, including stainless steel, Sheffield's most significant invention.

World steel supply was almost certain to outrun demand in the future, especially with modern steel making technology being exported to an ever increasing number of emerging economies. The likelihood was that these new plants would not only add to world supply of general steel but with the ability by some of them to melt increasingly sophisticated steels, it would be just a matter of time before they further threatened Sheffield's pre-eminence. As it was, much of what was re-rolled and forged in Sheffield was melted outside the area. Local works only melted a limited range of carbon, carbon manganese and silico-manganese steels, certainly not enough to meet local demand. Consequently, significant quantities of semi-finished steels were brought in to be finished by the city's smaller works. Tinsley bought much of its spring steel from Brymbo Steelworks, a part of the mighty Guest, Keen & Nettlefold Group. Their steel seldom gave cause for complaint, unlike some of the steel from the Scunthorpe area, which at times was very poor indeed. Steel from Sheffield could have been melted in Consett, Workington, Llanelli, Motherwell, Bilston, Briton Ferry, The Ruhr, or indeed Scunthorpe. Many a hand tool or garden implement proudly declaring *'Made of Sheffield Steel'* wasn't strictly true, except for the local contribution to added value.

Of the 120 or so local companies involved directly with the steel industry, the majority were small, independent, often family-based companies, operating within very specialised fields in which they had considerable expertise and would not require the large tonnages that the bigger firms needed. Some of these small companies were anarchic and others archaic, nonetheless they were a major factor in Sheffield's abilities to produce almost anything so long as it was in steel. It used to be said, tongue in cheek, that Sheffield was the world's greatest integrated steelworks, with almost every facility for steelworking and mostly, at a price, available for hire work. A number of Sheffield's small firms purported to be steel manufacturers: some, many years ago, may have been, but the 1960s were the heydays of the hire work trade and they had long since given up manufacturing anything except paperwork! It was pointless trying to compete with the major manufacturers on most commercial alloy grades but with some tool, stainless and special steels there could be a margin and, if there was, it would be exploited. It was perfectly feasible to have ingots melted, rolled, heat treated, ground, tested, packed, and finally despatched without the steel ever being touched by the seller, each operation being separately carried out by any one of a number of providers. Full knowledge of what was available for hire was of course essential in order to succeed - and succeed they did!

The constant transfer of steel throughout the city, on a daily basis, not only meant that as much steel was in transit as in any warehouse, but that a large transport infrastructure was also necessary. Many road hauliers existed on this toing and froing... some lorries seldom went beyond the City's boundaries yet provided their owners with a good living. Prompt and reliable service even with small or part loads was the key to this niche market and the recession of the early 1980s saw the end, not only of much of the steel industry, but also many of the local hauliers.

By the mid 1960s, Tinsley was one of the largest spring steel rollers in the country, with only three or four real competitors. Imports were not of any consequence and the automotive industry was not experiencing any undue foreign competition, although the success of the Mini which did not use conventional springs was something to ponder about, as was the increasing numbers of lorries with pneumatic suspension.

One of Tinsley's competitors was Rotherham Forge & Rolling Mills Co. Ltd. with whom we were not especially friendly. Another was J Beardshaw Limited, with whom we had a good relationship... 'not treading too often on one another's toes', was how Gilbert described the situation. He was a friend of their MD and the friendship extended down to both Sales Offices where mutual 'brain picking' was not discouraged. Beardshaw's had been established for over 250 years, employed 350 people and had a much wider range of products than Tinsley. Their Baltic Steelworks was a typical Sheffield Victorian, brick-built works. They had high frequency furnaces where a range of stainless and tool steels were melted as well as mills, forges, heat treatment plant and a saw shop. With this diversity, they had built up a very useful export trade but we encountered them most frequently in the spring trade. They were very constricted in the old Baltic Works and we had often, half-jokingly, thought that a merger of our companies would make some sense... especially as we reckoned on having the best mills. Therefore it came as a shock when they announced their merger with the much smaller Geo Senior Limited, of Ponds Forge in the middle of the City (the original Geo Senior had been a Tinsley Director as far back as 1897). None of it made much sense. Seniors were even more limited for space than Beardshaw's and though they doubtless now had access to a bigger forging and heat treatment facility than before, none of the moves seemed to have real logic. That is until Beardshaw Senior as they were now known, acquired an old mill at Sheepbridge in Chesterfield with room for expansion and plans to install a modern 'state of the art' mill with which they anticipated being able to dominate the spring steel trade.

Warning bells began to ring at Tinsley and the other spring steel rollers.

Chapter 6

POLITICS - NATIONALISATION

1 967 SAW UNEMPLOYMENT IN SHEFFIELD running at an average of 6,000 and with unfilled vacancies of some 2,000. Record outputs were being achieved at Templeborough, where Steel Peech & Tozer's recently modernised electric arc melting shop processed 26,500 tons in a week and English Steel Corporation's new Tinsley Park plant achieved 7,600 tons of alloy steel in a similar period. Throughout the area, production was running at a rate of 55,000 ingot tons a week, with only 70% of capacity being utilised.

Brown Bayley announced plans to install additional melting facilities at a cost of £1m which it was expected would be in operation by 1969. They already laid claim to having one of the most modern primary rolling mills in the country for the processing of alloy and stainless steels.

Hall & Pickles announced their merger with John Vessey & Sons Limited; Osborns announced their takeover of C R Denton Limited, as well as the merging of their castings business with Hadfields to form a new organisation to be known as Osborn-Hadfields with a new plant at Halfway.

Local company financial results for the previous year included: Firth Browns with a profit of £3,298,332; Arthur Lee & Sons - £948,883; Hadfields - £277,005; Balfour Darwins - £553,000; Brown Bayley - £153,171; Dunford Elliot - £210,209; and Tinsley Rolling Mills - £42,000.

Without doubt, it was the impending re-nationalisation of steel which created the greatest anticipation. With much opinion being less than favourable towards what was considered an unnecessary disruption of the industry, which was self-evidently not in a condition where State intrusion was necessary or generally welcome.

Sheffield, as a predominantly working class area, has a long tradition of supporting the Labour Movement. It was involved with the early Chartist and Syndicalist movements, as well as giving the world the term 'rattening', when used against workers who had become unpopular with the emerging 19th Century Trade Union movement. It therefore followed that there was a considerable measure of local support for the Labour Government of 1945 and their plans to bring steel into national ownership, as one of 'the means of production' in the Socialist agenda. But the steel industry in Sheffield was unique in the extent to which some of its large companies were also heavily engaged in areas other than the production of steel. Indeed, it had already been noted by early advocates of steel nationalisation, that Sheffield had a special position. 'The Socialisation of Iron & Steel! (Gollanz, 1946) points out the anomaly,

> *'Sheffield, therefore, must be considered alone and is better considered from the engineering angle than from that of steel. Sheffield is a steel consumer.'*

The Bill to nationalise steel was published in 1948 and disregarded any advice to look at Sheffield's situation in isolation. Consequently, Sheffield's biggest works were nationalised. However this was but a brief change in ownership for by October 1951, Labour no longer formed the Government, having lost the recent Election. Churchill's new administration had no intention of retaining the industry in Public Ownership and swiftly set about the task of de-nationalising steel. They established The Iron & Steel Holding & Realisation Agency which was charged with re-establishing effective private control, which they did, despite a few uncertainties and anxieties. Labour though, still retained the intention of nationalising the industry when they regained power.

Harold Wilson's Election victories of 1964 and 1966 brought with them the promise of *'The white heat of technological revolution'*, involving as it did the 'energising' and 'modernisation' of industry in order that the wider community could *'take charge of its destiny and no longer be ruled by market forces'*. Despite the grandiose words, Britain was a trading nation and market forces could never be removed from the equation.

The resulting *Iron & Steel Act* of 1967 nationalised all the country's steel plants, melting more than 500,000 ingot tons a year. This excluded some of the firms such as Firth Browns who had been included in the earlier measures, but included locally Samuel Fox, Park Gate, Steel Peech & Tozer, as well as English Steel Corporation with their important non-core interests as diverse as springs (which they also shared with Samuel Fox), engineers cutting tools, castings, heavy engineering and permanent magnets. Nationally, the new organisation, to be called British Steel Corporation, had only a small share of the low volume, high value products which Sheffield specialised in. Despite this, their influence over the industry would be very powerful and ultimately destructive.

With the dissolution of The Iron & Steel Board, their responsibility for determining prices for the industry fell into the hands of its biggest producer - British Steel Corporation. The remaining, independent companies formed the British Independent Steel Producers Association in an attempt to counterbalance the potentially monopolistic actions of the new giant and with its formation the usefulness of the old separate Associations vanished.

British Steel Corporation's first obvious impact upon their customers was a change in the appearance of the price schedules. The hands of the Marketing Department could be observed with, for the first time, pictures of the products on the books' covers. It was, as one puzzled steel buyer was heard to say, *'nice to know what they look like..... after all, I have only being buying bars for 20 years'!* They also changed the quality grading system on non-alloy steels leaving the onus on the customer to decide the levels of permissible defects they were prepared to accept. Gone forever were the terms; High Duty, Forging, Re-rolling, Deep Drawing Qualities - they had been replaced by a list of permissible defects from Grade I up to VII. It took a little time to get used to the system, but it probably proved to be an improvement on the old method. At least it cut down on arguments about what was a reasonable and permissible surface crack and what wasn't.

It appeared, to an outsider, that the management at English Steel Corporation had faired less well than their counterparts at United Steels, since most of the top jobs seemed to have gone the way of the so-called United Steels Mafia.

On a day-to-day basis nothing much changed. Old sales contacts remained, as did those for progress and technical support. Initially, the organisation was regionally based with Sheffield being the headquarters for its region based at the prestigious Mount - about as far away from a steelworks as you could get in Sheffield!

The creation of British Steel Corporation had given the country one of the world's largest steelmaking organisations and as befitted this position, it was to become policy that they would export a given quota, come what may.

At that time domestic demand was high, yet despite appeals from British manufacturers that they ensure the home market was satisfied before they attempted to meet their export quotas, they persisted in seeking export business. Some Europeans accused them of dumping, but that was a cry they all made about one another, but as delivery dates extended and steel became scarcer, many users in an attempt to maintain their own production, resorted to importing;

Fullwood Foundries
Craigneuk/Hallside/Tollcross
Scottish Fine Steels

Distington Foundries and Engineering

Taylor Bros.
Audenshaw
Openshaw

Brymbo

Wolverhampton
Birchley/Oldbury

Bilston

Landore Foundry
and Engineering

Panteg

Dock St

Stocksbridge
Park Gate
River Don
Ickles Press Forge Machine Shop
Grimesthorpe
Cyclops
Holme Lane
Renishaw Foundry
Steel Peech & Tozer
Tinsley Park

British Steel Corporation Special steels division sites.

sometimes they were shocked by what they received, for the steel may
well have been made in Scunthorpe or Teeside. Europeans were
buying British Steel and then reselling it back to the UK, sometimes
without even unloading the consignment, it having been bought and
sold on the high seas!

It was not only the question of their market priorities that caused
the rest of the industry concern; there were other matters which the
virtual monopoly position they now occupied gave rise to. British
Steel Corporation, at least in those areas in which they were active,
allowed them to effectively set the prices for the rest. The Chairman
of Firth Browns, Mr J M Clay, alluded to this when he voiced the
fears of the Independent producers, remarking that he hoped the

newly formed British Iron & Steel Producers Association would:

> *'provide a satisfactory means of communication with British Steel Corporation, since there is an apparent lack of an alternative to following the lead of British Steel Corporation in steel prices'.*

He further added,

> *'It is to be hoped that the British Steel Corporation will take steps to see that their selling prices are such, as to give a satisfactory return on the invested capital and thus permit the private sector to compete on equal terms'.*

These fears were real and in the event British Steel Corporation reduced certain prices, which perforce had to be matched by the smaller independents.

Some of the new sections Tinsley had undertaken to produce for the motor industry, were proving very difficult to roll satisfactorily on a regular basis. Unfortunately, for a company recognised as experts in the field, it was not easy to admit that they were unable to meet their customers' expectations. Despite pleas from the production staff to stop trying and wasting so much time and money, Gilbert Willis was adamant that they could and would be rolled. Finally, he had to submit and the troublesome door hinge section contract for the Ford Escort was abandoned. The whole event had been hugely disappointing and cost the company dear. It had made a loss in a year of £5,300 and in his statement to shareholders, Mr Gilbert Willis reported that;

> *'The Company had entered into a contract which had been calamitous and has since withdrawn'.*

There were, of course, other reasons for the losses the company had sustained and they could be attributed to a malign act by British Steel Corporation. Spring Steels were one product in which British Steel Corporation were not pre-eminent and in an act of mischief-making, they had reduced their prices. The very same Market Forces that Harold Wilson had earlier declared the wider community should *'no longer be ruled by'*, of course forced the independent re-rollers to match the reduction. That in itself was estimated to have cost £6,000. Clearly, the potential for British Steel Corporation to drive to the wall small firms by similar price cuts was a real one. The logic of merging interests was reinforced with this realisation and, observing the scene from afar, there existed a number of 'money merchants' who saw opportunities for themselves with the uncertainties being created by British Steel Corporation.

Dunford & Elliot were already controlled by a financier and in January 1968 they announced that they had offered to purchase the much bigger Hadfields Limited and create a new company, Dunford Hadfields. This was a case of a customer taking over a supplier and added to the merger momentum, given the realisation that small was no longer beautiful and the new world of steel could not support Sheffield's traditional collection of independent companies.

After three years it was time for British Steel Corporation to be reorganised and in March 1970 the corporation was split into six product groups. Sheffield's works were mainly within the new Special Steels Division with operations at Stocksbridge, Park Gate, River Don, The Ickles, Grimesthorpe, Cyclops, Holme Lane, Renishaw, Templeboro and Tinsley Park Works. New development was concentrating at Aldwarke and Thrybergh, while the old Park Gate Works were scheduled for closure, presaging the trend to turn steelworks' sites into shopping centres!

My immediate boss and friend, 'Bill' Holford was tragically killed in a road accident, ironically as he was returning from holiday to collect his 25 years' service award at the Cutlers Hall later the same day. I was appointed Sales Office Manager on the Monday morning and instructed to get rid of all signs of 'Bill' straight away. This we did. It seemed very callous at the time but in the event was probably correct. Life went on as did the speculation about who would take us over. Dunford-Hadfields seemed a likely suitor. Our works were almost adjacent, we bought some billets from them and we competed in some areas. Another likely option, or so we thought, would be a merger with Jonas Woodhead, who were one of our biggest customers and with whom relations were extremely good.

The summer of 1970 passed all too quickly. The Sales Office, with my two colleagues, had coped well with a record turnover and expanding export markets. I was increasingly accompanying Gilbert Willis on business trips and the occasional Conference, and enjoying the job. With my own house, car, wife and two lovely children, everything seemed rosy... except for the rumours that a nominee company were acquiring shares in Tinsley. Who were they buying on behalf of?

Beardshaw Senior had indeed built the very modern mill at Sheepbridge. It was rumoured to be occasionally highly productive, but that they were having the usual teething problems of getting it to perform well on a regular basis. The drain on the company resources was such that they were said to be experiencing financial problems.

No-one seemed to put much weight on these stories, but they evidently were true and very serious. It was a visibly shocked Gilbert Willis who broke the news to us that his old pal Michael Laycock and Beardshaw Senior Steels, had gone 'bust' and with them the livelihoods of some 500 employees. Life was not so rosy after all.

The episode had a deep effect on at least one of Tinsley's Directors. If an offer were to be made for Tinsley, it would be considered carefully. The prevailing circumstances of uncertainty about British Steel Corporation's future policies, together with the increasing difficulties of a small company financing its own future modernisation programme, made merger more likely. The shareholders' interests were paramount: Gilbert Willis had no intention of suffering Beardshaw's fate.

The Sheepbridge Mill, which had contributed so much to Beardshaw's problems, was eventually bought by Dunford-Hadfields, who would in time master it and realise its full productive potential. Baltic Steelworks still exist, but all that remains of Ponds Forge is the stone arch, proudly bearing the name of its original owners and now incorporated into the structure of Sheffield's Ponds Forge International swimming complex. Interestingly, one of the base blocks from the forge was too heavy to be removed easily and that too was incorporated as an architectural feature.

Chapter 7

UNLIKELY BEDFELLOWS

FATE SEEMS TO HAVE A HABIT of bringing together strange bedfellows, common interest often outweighing mutual distrust and by submerging petty self-interests creates a vital new relationship. Humankind's history is littered with such events. Military and religious alliances are just such examples. Sometimes though, fate can be cruel and the new partnership can be as destructive as a bad marriage.

Tinsley and Rotherham Forge did not enjoy a close business relationship. Tinsley staff felt they were not to be trusted. They broke agreements. In short, we had as little to do with them as possible, but...they were our biggest competitor and the mysterious buyer of Tinsley's shares, had designs which could affect us both.

Rotherham Forge & Rolling Mills Co Ltd was founded in 1893 but could lay claim to a much older ancestry, going back to 1754. In that year the Earl of Effingham granted a lease for a piece of land in the manor of Kimberworth to a group of local men. William Fairbank's plan described the land as being '*at the head of Rotherham Mill Weyre*' and known as Forge Island. It was in many respects similar to the site Dyson & Shirt would choose for their mill and was presumably chosen for much the same reasons. The Don had recently been canalised and Forge Island was 'twixt river and cut'.

The lease, signed on the -

> '*29th day of September in the 28th year of our Sovereign Lord George II was between Thos. Earl of Effingham deputy Earl Marshall of England and Saml. Walker of Masboro, Iron founder and Aaron Walker of Masboro, Jonathan Walker of Grenoside in the Parish of Ecclesfield and Jonathan Crawshaw of the same place*'.

The Walkers are numbered amongst the area's pioneering industrialists and their business associations extended to partnerships with others of their contemporaries including the Roebucks, who in 1770 had introduced the first real Bank to Sheffield, and John Booth of The Brushes. The three of them formed a partnership in 1750 'to convert iron into steel'. Obviously, the lease of land by the Earl was for an entirely different venture, and the Walkers did not stay too long at Forge Island. Over the next 100 years, the lease was re-assigned on several occasions and the forge was known variously as Liversidge & Crownshaw; Knowles & Brown; Brown & Sons; G & J Brown, before finally becoming a joint stock company with the title Rotherham Forge & Rolling Mills Company Limited. By that time they were not only carrying on the traditional pursuits at Forge Island, but were also supplying rolled bars.

The world's first solid railway engine tyre was produced at the works, based on the patent of Heppenstall, the works blacksmith and in 1938 the steam hammer on which it had been manufactured was demolished to make way for a modern hydraulic press. The original forge base block, weighing 80 tons and made in 1860 was broken up on site by the use of 80 shots of dynamite - to the alarm of local residents. Little wonder that they left the block at Ponds Forge in situ!

In the same year, with re-armament already underway, the Chairman reported to shareholders that the Company was fully employed and had produced a record turnover but that they were having difficulty in obtaining steel supplies. He paid tribute to the workforce whom he described as the 'best' and as well as increasing the amount to be paid into the Pension Fund also announced the introduction of a week's paid holiday for every employee as thanks for their efforts and as a share in the Company's prosperity.

The small scale of production of many of our early iron and steel works meant that the restrictions imposed by 'island' sites, typified by both Wharf Lane and Forge Lane, were not an undue hindrance, but as demand increased, their limitations started to impose penalties in production. Tinsley had sought out room for expansion as early as 1914, but Rotherham was more tardy. Not until 1960 did they announce a £750,000 plan to move the entire plant, over a 10 year period, to Greasboro Street. The Rotherham Corporation gave every encouragement for the move, which involved the demolition of over 200 houses. They had a noisy plant, occupying a prime position in the town centre, but it would be many more years before cinema-goers would be able to relax, free from the boom of the hammers. The smoke problems, created by the many coal-fired furnaces, had largely been removed with conversion to gas as early as 1951. Tinsley would retain coal firing for some of their mills until the late 1960s, but they were not surrounded by domestic and commercial properties, and the problem was less pressing. Unfortunately, Rotherham Corporation never agreed a purchase price for the site, merely arriving at an understanding. This would become a source of some bitterness.

Rotherham Forge produced a set of excellent results for the year ended 31 March 1967 which reflected the strength of their export trade which had been carefully built up over many years. They had a much bigger and more diverse trade than Tinsley which was apparent from their results. Turnover was £2,262,258 of which export amounted to £524,613. Profit for the year was £129,247. This result was at a time when the country was being again urged to 'export or die', in an effort to reduce the crippling balance of payments difficulties, which were to blight the country's economic situation for many more years. Congratulations on Rotherham's export achievements were received from the town's well-liked Member of Parliament, Brian O'Malley, on a visit to see the progress of the move to the new Works. Not only was export possible, but it was also profitable!

On 4 September 1969, Rotherham received an unexpected proposal with the announcement by Oliver Jessel, the great grandson of Marcus Samuel of Hill Samuel the merchant bankers and now one of a new breed of financiers that the 1960s had spawned, that he intended bidding for the Company's Ordinary Share Capital of £425,000. Rotherham's 5s shares were currently dealing at 6s 6d. and Leeds Assets', Jessel's take-over vehicle, offer valued the Company at only £500,000. The *Sheffield Star* interviewed Jessel about the bid. He remarked, 'If the talks are successful, I don't expect it would involve any redundancies'. Not for the first time would these assurances be given regarding livelihoods being put at risk in the search for individual profit. He also added that Rotherham Forge would benefit from access to greater funds and from being a part of a larger organisation: comforting words indeed to the Chairman, Col. Ralph Hodgson, whose initial reaction to the bid was that,

'the obvious thing is that if this comes through, instead of having a large number of shareholders, we should be a member of a large group with more resources. I would expect that the Company would go on exactly as before, but would be stronger and not on its own.'.

By 27 September, the penny had dropped; the offer was not a good one and the Board advised its shareholders to reject it since,

'the industrial logic for merger was not readily apparent. One of the main objects (of the offer) is to gain control of Rotherham's assets cheaply'.

Jessel though had an industrial logic for making the offer. The nominees who had been acquiring Tinsley's shares had been doing so, on his behalf, for later use. As for the Company's assets, they had a site, centrally placed, which would soon become redundant. How much would it be worth, given the excellent prospects for redevelopment?

On 11 October a revised offer of about £1m, of Leeds Assets 'Loan Stock' was submitted and despite the absence of a cash alternative, the Directors recommended acceptance. The financier admitted that the Directors had only been doing their job by sticking out for a better offer and that he had no bad feelings about them. He visited his acquisition and confessed to being impressed with what he had seen of the Company's operations.

The Chairman, as well as the Managing Director, as a result of re-organisations, resigned within 6 months of the takeover and thus ended any local control over the company. Frank Gardner was deputed by Jessel to carry out a wholesale investigation of the Company's organisation and methods. He gathered an assortment of 'specialists' from Leeds Assets and between them they embarked upon sweeping changes. The effect of these changes was to put the direction of the organisation firmly into the hands of a growing band of Financial and Management Accountants. In the short term, financial results were good, half time profits quadrupled, and the new owners were expressing great confidence in the future.

Gordon Jones was appointed Managing Director and he quickly shocked Rotherham Corporation by announcing that the Company would not now be leaving the Forge Lane site. He reinforced this by saying that he ...

'could not allow assets to remain under-utilised and, as a consequence, the drop stamp would be recommissioned as quickly as possible'.

He felt quite justified in these actions, especially as no price had ever been agreed for the sale of the land to the Corporation.

27 November 1970 brought a further shock, with the announcement that Rotherham Forge was making an agreed bid for the Ordinary Shares of Tinsley. That evening, several members of Tinsley's staff were asked to stay behind and mail the offer documents to shareholders. It felt like helping make the rope with which you would hang yourself! Of all the possibilities we had talked about, this one seemed about the worst possible. Tales of what had happened to Rotherham staff in their re-organisation had percolated through and created some alarm, but Gordon Jones was reckoned to be a decent sort. Jessel's industrial logic was becoming much clearer.

Tinsley's Board appeared to have concluded a much better deal than had Rotherham's. Jessel was proposing to offer 25s 6d of Rotherham unsecure Loan Stock for every 10s ordinary share, making the offer worth £815,000. At least Tinsley's shareholders would get something out of the deal unlike Beardshaws who had been forced into liquidation. The shareholders' interests were paramount and as the Willis family controlled around 22% of the ordinary shares, Gilbert Willis no doubt felt justified in recommending acceptance. Even the local British Iron, Steel and Kindred Trade Association representative Alec Hogg, expressed confidence in the future for his members - although at the same time remarking that the Unions had not been consulted.

Tinsley had made a profit of £195,000 in the year to 31 June 1970, without the dubious benefit of reorganisation, and as an expression of thanks, the Company had decided that everyone would go to Amsterdam for a weekend. This went ahead, the following May, and was the last time we were to meet as a Group.

Chapter 8

BEGINNING OF THE END

DECEMBER 1970 WAS SPENT, by everyone on the staff, pondering the future. We had all been reassured that we would 'do alright' and that we were as good at our jobs as any at Greasboro Street. But it was the end of an era and we all knew it. Little empires and routines would be destroyed and the familiar surroundings which helped create the feelings of security were to be uprooted. I had changed jobs briefly, in my time at Tinsley and was of an age group which appreciated change, but for many on the staff it was a daunting prospect.

A rainy January morning in 1971 saw my Sales Office being transferred to Greasboro Street: one of the first steps in the merger was to be the combination of the Sales functions. My new role was to be Export Sales Office Manager, with a staff of five and an export trade of nearly £1m annually. It was a little daunting. Gilbert Willis would be Chairman and Gordon Jones, who much later would be knighted for his services to the water industry, retained his position as Managing Director. Amongst a number of other Directors, John Neale became responsible for production at the three sites of Greasboro Street, Wharf Lane and Forge Lane. My immediate 'superior' was the Sales Director, John Lund, an old Rotherham 'hand' who had survived the recent reorganisations. He was a pleasant man who appeared to be carrying the cares of the world on his shoulders. Patient and considerate, he appeared an anachronism when compared with some of Jessel's new recruits who strutted around the offices, careless of the world they were helping destroy. The new Company, to be known as Rotherham-Tinsley Steels Limited, had combined net assets of £2m, a turnover of £6^{1}/2m annually, employed 900 people and would consume 80,000 tons of steel per annum. The merger of these hitherto competing companies was only a part of Jessel's logic; the consumption of so much steel made them an attractive proposition for his next move. Meanwhile, they could legitimately claim their position as 'the leading British re-roller of spring steel bars for both laminated and coil springs for the railway, motor and general engineering trades'. They had eight hot rolling mills and five cold rolling mills producing a wide range of carbon and alloy steels. Apart from springs, typical uses for their

NICKEL CHROME MOLYBDENUM
NICKEL CHROME
NICKEL

NICKEL MANGANESE MOLYBDENUM
NICKEL MOLYBDENUM

WE SUPPLY
STAMPINGS, BARS,
SHEETS
& FORGINGS

A L L O Y

S T E E L S

IN THESE
QUALITIES

MANGANESE MOLYBDENUM
MANGANESE MOLYBDENUM CHROME
MANGANESE NICKEL MOLYBDENUM

CARBON CHROME
CHROME VANADIUM
CHROME MOLYBDENUM

TRADE ROFCO MARK

Rotherham Forge brochure, showing cross sections of some of the many special purpose steel bars produced. (opposite)

Manufacturers of Steel of all kinds for Agricultural Engineers

SPECIALITY :

BEATER·PLATES

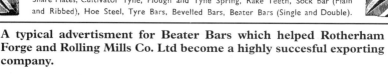

Also Steel for the following purposes :
Sheets for Plough Plates (Solid and Soft Centre) pared to shape, also for Chaff Knives,
Reaper Knives (Planished), Scythe Sheets (Curved or Straight), Discs for Coulters,
Share Plates, Cultivator Tyne, Plough and Tyne Spring, Rake Teeth, Sock Bar (Plain
and Ribbed), Hoe Steel, Tyre Bars, Bevelled Bars, Beater Bars (Single and Double).

A typical advertisement for Beater Bars which helped Rotherham Forge and Rolling Mills Co. Ltd become a highly succesful exporting company.

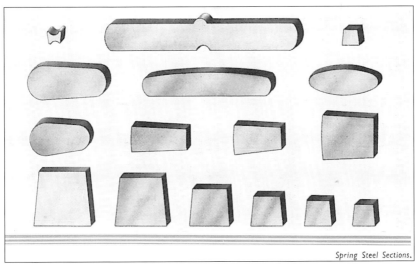

Spring Steel Sections.

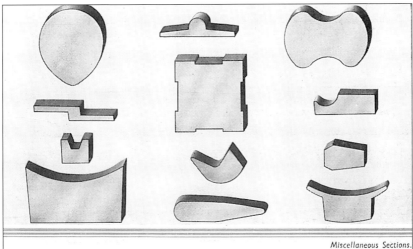

Miscellaneous Sections.

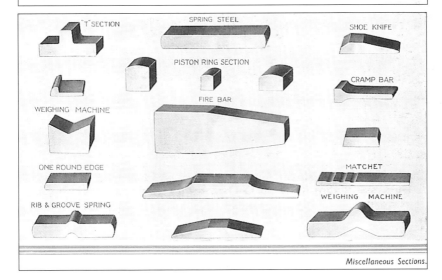

Miscellaneous Sections.

products were: edge tools (forks, augers, axes, picks, hammers, garden shears); agricultural engineering (plough plates, chaff knives, sickles, scythes, cultivator tines, sock bars, beater bars, coulter discs), aircraft steels, steels for the textile trade, spindle steels, saw plates, mining drill steel, shoe and paper knife steels, file steels, cutlery steels, machete steels, composite steels, vehicle wheel rim and lock ring sections.

As well as the rolling mills, they had a large and versatile drop forge producing stampings for the motor, agricultural and general engineering trades and an extensive machine shop which was capable of producing fully machined forgings of up to 12 tons in weight. They specialised in producing marine, diesel and generator crankshafts.

Both companies had built up a vast amount of experience within their specialities. This exhibited itself with the differing mill set-ups, rolling and cooling temperatures that the myriad sizes, sections and steel qualities entailed. Rotherham had pursued the manufacturing of composite iron and steel products which Tinsley had allowed to decline. These steels could be hot or cold finished; could be rolled in either the bar or sheet mills. Each billet or slab, before rolling, required to be individually machined to incorporate the insert of a different quality; with every section requiring a unique form being machined out of the main backing stock. An old brochure identified 28 standard forms and there were of course many non-standard sections which were rolled.

These two old companies had differing approaches to creating a successful industrial recipe. The new owners added to these recipes, uncertainty, distrust, inexperience and ultimately, muddle. Evidence of any planning for the day-to-day workings of the new company were difficult to observe. Sales and pricing policies were sometimes at odds and it appeared that an approach of 'suck it and see' permeated the policy-making process. Shortly after the takeover, in an interview given to *The Observer*, Jessel had remarked that he had acquired both of the companies for '*bus tickets, and used ones at that*'. That was exactly how it appeared to his employees. He cared little for steel, traditional values or indeed, even bus tickets.

A lack of product knowledge not only affected the Sales function, even some of the production staff lacked detailed knowledge of a number of specialised products. This would have serious consequences in the not-too-distant future. A little knowledge would indeed be a dangerous thing - but with a management style which looked upon change as a veritable asset, those with only a little knowledge would soon be the only ones left! This inevitably led to the wrong products being made from the wrong materials and delivered to the wrong customers on the wrong day with the wrong prices. A heavy price to pay for the hasty merging of two Companies!

Despite evidence to the contrary, the Company put out a statement, which appeared in *The Rotherham Advertiser* on 5 March 1971, stating that: 'The management of both companies is now fully integrated'.

Much of what Rotherham produced was unfamiliar to me. I knew very little about forging, which, perhaps fortunately, was something for which we had little export demand. The period was one where everyone tried to become familiarised with new products, new customers and new markets. Rotherham rolled some fairly unique products; some seemed on the point of obsolescence, some were indeed obsolete. Nevertheless, if there was a profit margin they would still be produced. Composite iron and steel, if only to my inexperienced eye, seemed just such a product. Time-consuming to produce and with many processes to be carried out before it was finished, it was asking to be replaced by newer technology - which was indeed happening abroad. This new technology would be just as reliable as the old but infinitely cheaper. Of greater long-term

Typical products of composite iron and steel. The dark section being the harder tool steel insert while the pale part is the much softer and hence more flexible and easily machined 'backing', mild steel.

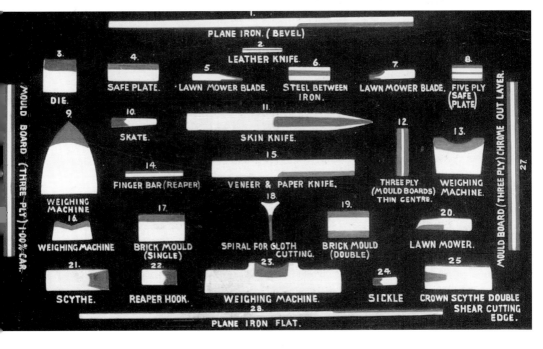

Machine straightening of beater bars.

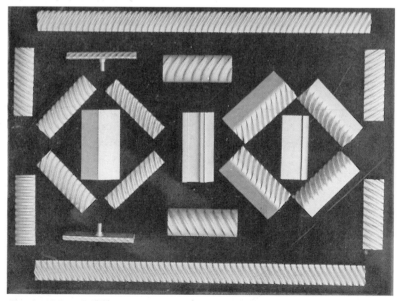

A selection of different Beater Bar sections.

significance to the Company and its successors was the production of Beater Bars, (sometimes known as Rasp Bars). Rotherham was one of a small number of companies world-wide who could roll this complicated and very necessary part of every combined harvester.

The story of how they came to be in this position may be apocryphal - but it has the ring of truth. It appeared that there was a mill in Germany which had perfected the rolling techniques needed to produce a number of new designs. This they had done before the outbreak of war in 1939, and they had jealously guarded their roll designs, which were the vital element of their success. With the war eventually reaching a climax and Allied Forces occupying the collapsing Third Reich, a small group of British Intelligence Officers, in a fast mobile column, advanced toward their objective, which happened to be a certain German rolling mill. Avoiding German resistance, the column 'liberated' all of the Beater Bar roll designs which then 'found' their way to Rotherham. Apocryphal or not, the staff of Rotherham Forge was very soon producing them and also by utilising their powerful position building very lucrative export markets.

Both the Americans and the Russians had the ability to produce some of the designs, but Rotherham was uniquely placed in having them all. This treasure was well guarded. They not only rolled the steel which was sold to most of the manufacturers, but also established a market, internationally, for spares. These they assembled in a small part of the works: drilled, welded, painted and assembled in 'balanced' sets they were exported world-wide. Small wonder that Brian O'Malley had been impressed with their export performance! As steel is rolled, so the mill rolls wear and the profile becomes larger. Adjustments are regularly made to keep the finished steel within tolerance, but eventually a new set of rolls will have to be introduced. Roll changing is a costly exercise and is always kept to a minimum. Experience will dictate when the procedure is carried out. Beater Bars are a three dimensional product, roll wear is consequently greater than with a normal section. It is also essential that finished bars are consigned from a limited period of 'time' in any rolling, so as to minimise the inconvenience to the customer of assembling a 'Beater Drum' which is out of balance. Over the years, Rotherham had perfected a system which gave very satisfactory results.

The new owners questioned the validity of most things, and in the race to squeeze extra profit, they hit on the notion of reducing roll changing time by avoiding it until absolutely necessary. They added to the 'felony' by dispensing with the practice of 'time' segregation. The initial results were a spectacular improvement in output and thus profit. Mammon had been served yet again...or had he?

In a matter of a few weeks, the complaints started to be received from customers. They were, as some had predicted, having trouble in balancing the drums. What had we done to alter years of almost perfection? No-one dared tell them. This was not an isolated incident but typical. Inexperienced managers who chose to ignore experienced advice were a daily part of Rotherham-Tinsley's early days. Sales forecasts were wildly optimistic and once given were a justification for a spate of interesting foreign trips carried out by senior management as well as a rush to replace office equipment. For a while, the old staff in Management Accounts had been preaching that the new system as introduced by Jessel was producing false, inaccurate information. Being old in years, their advice went unheeded and the 'ship' carried on blissfully ignorant of the truth.

Chapter 9

MODERNISATION

YOUNG PEOPLE, IN GENERAL, have less experience of life and as a consequence are much more receptive to newer business dogmas, especially those of which they have little knowledge. It is always a useful concept to question the wisdom that others have learned for there may well be more than one solution to a problem. But, do all new brooms sweep clean; and, if they do, how much that is worth keeping gets thrown away as well? Sheffield's steel industry was very often guilty of staying for too long with the old tried and tested methods, relying too often on manpower, which could be got rid of more easily than investing in modern technology which might at times be under-utilised. There were, of course, exceptional companies whose plant was as modern as any, but they were indeed the exception and certainly not the rule. Full order books usually blinded management to the newer, more efficient methods which were being adopted abroad. Rotherham's 'Iron and Steel' products were an example of a company not being aware of the new technologies and relying for too long on the merits of their old

Typical agricultural products including 'Mould boards' being prepared for further treatment. This is the component which turns the earth over. The arrowhead shaped piece is the cutting point of the ploughshare. The circular item is a 'Coulter Disc' which in use forms a 'Disc Harrow', which further breaks down the soil after ploughing.

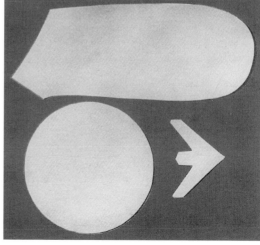

system which was eminently satisfactory but expensive to operate.

The technique of welding ferrous metals together, under conditions of heat and pressure, had been perfected by Rotherham Forge over many years. Iron and steel could be produced in many forms, but the biggest demand was in the form of thin plates. These plates consisted of, usually, two outer layers of a high carbon or alloy steel with the centre plate being a soft mild steel (originally it would have been wrought iron). The concept gave flexibility as well as toughness and wear resisting properties, which was an essential requirement in a plough plate, or 'mould-board'. Rotherham had rolled many thousands of tons, much of which had 'added value', by being supplied to customers cut to the pattern of the board. The actual manufacturing process was time-consuming and thus costly. It involved the elimination of surface rust by shot blasting the thin slabs. These in turn were assembled in the correct order and finally wrapped in very thin steel sheet. This wrapping of the assembly was an important part of the process, as it reduced the possibility of furnace gases oxidising the plates and inhibiting the welding process. Under strict temperature conditions the whole assembly would then be rolled out to the required thickness and width, the thin layer of covering material being so heavily oxidised that it would fall off as 'mill scale'.

Under the Jessel mode of management, everything was in question. So ill-versed were they with the 'feel for steel', that usually the wrong questions were asked. In an effort to improve profit, by increasing output and reducing the costs of preparing the slabs, it was decided to dispense altogether with the wrapping process. Of course, experience indicated that the end result would be a failure, but the old hands had learned to let them get on with it, since no notice would be taken of their advice anyway. The growing pile of very thin sheets - a result of the failure to weld together - was ample proof that nothing in the old, tried and tested method, was done for the fun of it. The question that ought to have been asked was, could the same results of a well-made iron and steel mould board be obtained by a different method?

Sales of these plates had become very poor in Norway, which traditionally had been a good market. It was decided that I should meet a colleague in Copenhagen and then fly on to Stavanger to meet our agent and arrange a series of visits to our erstwhile customers.

We visited our principal Norwegian customer Kvaerner's, main factory and soon discovered the reason why our orders had dried up. Someone had asked the right question and come up with another and cheaper answer. They had built a new factory almost, along the entire shore of a fjord. Ships moored at one end of the factory unloaded their cargo of steel then moved to the other end of the factory and reloaded with finished machinery. Between the Norwegians and their German suppliers they had developed and invested in a method whereby all the attributes of traditional iron and steel three-ply could be achieved by flame hardening. Not only was the end product as good, it was also much cheaper, and with the economy of scale the new plant permitted, it did not take long to recognise the threat to our entire market. We had been caught 'with our pants down' and we were going to suffer the consequences. In the future this would happen all too frequently to the Sheffield steel trade, which was throughout, too complacent. Not only were the steel manufacturers infected with this other 'English Disease', our customers were suffering equally from the condition, the first symptom of which is short-sighted decision making. Some of Sheffield's agricultural implement manufacturers would have found the museum of old machinery which Kvaerner ran, as well-equipped as many of their production plants.

The German steel industry had, during the last War, actively pursued the development of steels using alternative alloying strategies in an attempt to reduce their dependence on strategic metals. In this they had largely been successful and it appeared that the steel Kvaerner were buying used a small addition of Boron to give the desired results. We obtained the specification and determined that on our return to the UK we would try and get a quotation from British Steel Corporation for the steel. If the Germans could make it, then so should we.

We were very late arriving back home. Our return to the office next morning was heralded with the unexpected visit of Oliver Jessel. The car park was empty; this was a certain indicator that his Bell Jetranger would be on its way. It duly arrived, to be followed a little while later by a convoy of his 'mercenaries'. Whilst we had been away, there had been a crisis and a full Board Meeting had been hurriedly called. My immediate boss appeared, ashen-faced, from the meeting an hour or so later, and asked if I would see him in his office as soon as possible. I was greeted by his normally rather fussy secretary who now appeared anxious. He explained that instead of the Company running in profit, it had in fact incurred losses. This was not really a surprise since the only staff who had believed the Management Accounts were those who were preparing them. The old cost accountants had been advising that the new system was flawed, but like most others, their opinions had been disregarded. Price lists had been abandoned; everything was given a cost, which was sometimes erroneous, and too many orders had been taken on which only made a contribution to overheads. The net result was that the mix of products being rolled had gone out of balance. Higher prices which were charged for some profitable lines had resulted in cancelled orders and there had been an influx of very marginal items. As a consequence of these losses, remedial action had been taken and my Sales Director would be retiring and virtually everyone over the age of 40 would be made redundant with the loss of around 100 jobs. He asked me not to think of going until after he had gone. He was tired of the new Management and really wanted to get away and if I were to leave they might ask him to stay on. Jessel's growing empire, was built around public and financial confidence and in order that this was maintained he had to be seen to be acting positively.

On 1st September 1971, it was announced that, as a result of a sudden shortage of orders, the $10\frac{1}{2}''$ mill at Greasboro Street would be closing, but the job losses affected more than this one mill. So much for the confidence which had been expressed less than a year earlier.

The loss of a job could never be adequately compensated for by the payment of redundancy money. The individual's sense of loss and of belonging is destroyed and society as a whole shares in the suffering. These relatively small job losses would be a harbinger of future events for the area's steel industry, as sometimes inept and often selfish managements failed to respond in a concerted manner to a changing world.

Not only did the Sales Director go, but Gordon Jones and Gilbert Willis appeared to take extended leave, never to re-appear in the Company. Jessel sent his No. 1 troubleshooter, a man whose reputation, of Wild West proportions, travelled before him. Frank Gardner, whose team of 'experts' had originally introduced the malevolent management system, returned to make it work. Famed for his wearing of yellow braces, this apparel was to become a ceremonial gift to all male members of staff who left in the future. So poor was morale by this time that Frank Gardner issued a notice to the effect that he was tired of seeing long faces and in the future he expected, Stalin like, to see happy faces as we went about our work. He had the reputation of a ruthless operator, but he did have the virtue of at times being prepared to listen and ask for opinions. It is a pity that these virtues had been less apparent in his earlier visit. 'Maximise effort in those areas where profit could be maximised' became his clarion call, as did his explanation for not taking too many sudden alterations to the course of business. He likened business to flying an aircraft. Movement on the joystick may not result in an instant change in direction, but too much will certainly result in a stall. Panic measures were almost always disastrous. Unfortunately, these sentiments had not prevailed earlier in the Company's life, and more change had been a part, or so it seemed, of Company policy.

The redundancies left a very inexperienced staff coming across problems for which they did not have ready answers. I became an 'expert' on Beater Bars, something about which, truthfully, I had only a limited knowledge. Nor was I well versed in a number of export market requirements. In the recent past I would have consulted my Sales Director, but now it was a matter all too often of finding out the hard way...with sometimes painful results. No sooner had we recovered from another office move than rumours started to circulate about another merger. Somewhat mendaciously, we were told there would be no more changes, but my sources revealed that discussions were underway with Brown Bayley Steels. Now, if this was true, Jessel's industrial logic was revealing itself again and a merger made very good sense indeed. The 80,000 tons of steel a year Rotherham-Tinsley consumed was something worth controlling. The problem though seemed to be that Brown Bayleys had never been suppliers for the larger part of the qualities we were buying!

They were a much larger organisation than Rotherham-Tinsley, employing around 3,000 people on a site of over 40 acres in Attercliffe, Sheffield. They melted, rolled and forged alloy and stainless steels. In the past we had bought relatively small quantities of billet from them and they were certainly not one of our major suppliers in any sense. They could, doubtless, supply a large portion of our requirements

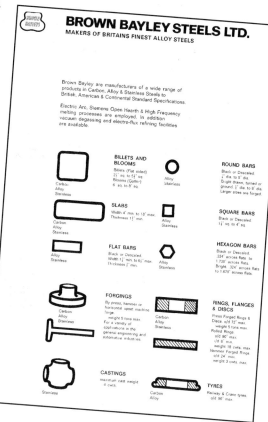

Part of the Brown Bayleys Steels Ltd. range of special purpose alloy steels and the forms in which they could be produced.

for silico-manganese steel but what of the remaining, often low value purchases?

I had visited Brown Bayleys on a few occasions. There were obvious visible signs of recent investment, but the over-riding impression was one of a fairly dirty and untidy place, with too much mill scale underfoot to ever have kept Gilbert Willis happy. They were the smallest of Sheffield's 'Big Four', with a capacity of around 160,000 Tons and their shares were currently controlled by a Government Quango, the Industrial Reorganisation Corporation, whose nominee, Tom Kilpatrick, a well-known local figure, was in charge. Jessel was now being viewed as the 'sole catalyst of Private Sector Rationalisation in Sheffield', and, when, on 23 December 1971, the announcement of the takeover was made public, it hardly came as a surprise. Tom Kilpatrick announced that '*after a short period of negotiation it had been agreed that Brown Bayley Steels Ltd would be taking over Rotherham Tinsley Steels*' a new Company which had existed independently for less than a year. Acknowledging fears over job security he declared that '*there would be no wielding of the big hatchet*'. The logic of the move was two-fold. Firstly, Brown Bayley would obtain a very substantial customer whilst also widening their product range; and, secondly, with Jessel receiving an estimated £1,500,000, he had in effect got his money back and still retained 25% of a much bigger company. Logic indeed, and an answer to Rotherham's Board, who could see no industrial logic in his offer two years earlier. Early results of the takeover saw some investment being spent on modernisation at both Wharf Lane and Greasboro Street.

This was one merger too much for me and I determined to move. As it was, the situation would only last for some two years before the new arrangements would be disrupted once again.

Chapter 10

RECYCLING

I HAD SPENT A FEW YEARS AWAY from Tinsley in the late 1960s, working for both a local steel stockholder and a national steel merchant. My experiences at both companies had been useful ones. I had learned that there were only fundamentally two types of merchant; the honest ones and the others.

Much of what I had learned from 'Bill' Baldwin, who was my manager whilst at Geo. Cohen Sons & Co Ltd, was to prove useful in the future. Cohens were a large organisation, both nationally and internationally based with interests in ferrous and non-ferrous scraps, machine tools, plant hire, dismantling and reusable steels. They were, along with Thos. W Ward and Cox & Danks, among the biggest of their kind sharing as they did many of the contracts for the disposal of materials from, among others, British Rail. Much of this, at the time, consisted of old rails, wagons and locomotives. There had always been a tradition of the steel industry re-using or perhaps more correctly recycling as much as it could and the industry had a high rate of recovery. The open hearth and electric furnaces used scrap as their feed stock but Bill Baldwin's function was to get the local mills and forges to buy as much reusable steel as he could.

Tinsley Rolling Mills amongst others had for many years used scrap and surplus Bull Head rails for by slitting them, then re-rolling the base and the head they could be turned into flat bars. Locomotive tyre, when trimmed and cut to suitable weights, was rolled into sheets for the eventual manufacture of agricultural implements. So good was the quality of these steels that Massey Ferguson among others wrote their steel specification for 'Coulter discs' around cross rolled engine tyre. Even Kayser had admitted to Harry Brearley, that his fortune had been made by re-using engine tyre. It was a local, tried and tested practice which lasted until both the hand mills and the steam locomotives became redundant.

Railway axles were another useful reusable railway component for which there was always a ready market, with both the re-rollers as well as some of the forges. An axle is made of high grade steel generally with a carbon composition of 0.30/.35% but it was not unknown, after testing, to find the odd ancient wrought-iron axle with a carbon composition of up to 0.45%. After chemical analysis, the axles were carefully segregated in accordance with the test results and then bundled for delivery to a mill or a forge. Mostly they went to a rolling mill where they would be processed into bars or billets. A rolling mill is non-productive whilst changing rolls, which might last for several hours. Rather than earn nothing, a number of local mills undertook this 'rough' work as a filler and very useful for everyone it was. Jonas & Colver, were one of the major recipients and many thousands of tons of axles were rolled by them to end up as chains, hammers, stampings, and general engineering bars.

The steam locomotive was also recycled by the further use of its smoke tubes, and superheater tubes as well as connecting rods. Of course what could not be reused, was put to scrap.

It ought perhaps to be remembered that for much of the 1950s to 1970s, there were significant periods of steel shortage and in 1963 it was estimated that 230,000 tons of reusable steels were being utilised within the UK. The re-usable trade satisfied a real need. The ship breakers provided scrap propeller shafts. These could be scrapped in multiples since all the shafts from a given vessel would normally be disposed of simultaneously. Ship shafts, which could be very large often weighing in excess of 10 tons, were eagerly sought after and generally expected to be profitable. It was always a priority to obtain a rough sketch or, better still, a drawing of the shaft showing if it still retained its gun metal lining. This, once removed, could be a very profitable part of the shaft, especially if it had been estimated in the weight as steel! There were ready markets with forges and stockholders for almost all the shafts that became available. Many a stockholder who today proudly holds quality certification, made his mark in the seconds and reusable trade and none more so than those who specialise in holding stocks of large diameter bars.

During my short time at Cohens, all manner of Government establishments and companies disposed of surplus stocks. The realisation of capital that was tied up in old stocks, brought with it a usual windfall to the relatively few companies who were in the market and could afford to pay immediately for their purchases. Cohens were in such a position and were approved to receive Tenders from many diverse organisations; British Rail, Ministry of Defence, The Admiralty. We were offered all manner of items - Sten Guns (minus firing pins), cannon shells, tin helmets, horseshoes, diesel locomotives, cockpit canopies and, of course, steel. This might consist of anything from 'clog iron' to perhaps the latest sophisticated nickel alloys. Whatever it was we tried to sell it... and usually did. As Bill Baldwin used to say *'any fool can sell steel, but you need to be really clever to always know where to buy it'.*

All steelworks make mistakes... sometimes they are referred to as surpluses, sometimes as seconds. Access to the works lists containing details of these would make a few individuals very rich but they were never widely issued and truthfully this encouraged a less than open relationship between supplier and purchaser. Cohens had their connections or perhaps it would be more correct to say that Bill Baldwin had his contacts. Park Gate Iron & Steel were completing the modernisation of their melting plant with the usual teething problems, and Cohens won the contract to clear their works of trial materials. A regular supply of 7 inch sq, low alloy, blooms came by way of the contract and these in turn were disposed of to a number of local forges. Some reusable merchants were happier dealing with the more acceptable forms of steel recycling - second hand plates, girders and tubes - but with others there was always a temptation to work the oracle and turn 'a sow's ear into a silk purse'. Some unscrupulous merchants took great risks.

Test and chemical analysis certificates, those essential documentary proofs, could and were sometimes altered, without thought of the possible consequences to third parties. The more responsible merchants, were aware of the consequences of manipulating test results and the practice was frowned upon, but greed and blindness to the consequences ensured that it did happen. No matter how good any system is, if there is sufficient incentive to breach the regulations, they will be breached.

Reusable steels 'found' their way into some nationally important organisations, including at least one Ordnance Factory, having been rolled from some 7 inch sq. blooms of Park Gate origin. The steel merchants who were based in the Midlands were especially good at inferring a steel's grade by its surface appearance. A common statement was that if the steel was 'blue' it was 'prime'. When spoken in the 'Brummy' drawl, this simplistic view of the possible defects the steel might contain, was intended to be reassuring. With few regulations the real urge, coupled with ample opportunity to make money, usually outweighed the other considerations, more especially since those who seemed to possess the least amount of technical knowledge and integrity, were generally making bigger profits. Steel was, so we were advised, just another product to sell - like biscuits! Sheffield was being taken over by biscuit salesmen. They had none of the feeling, and had never absorbed the mystique of steel. Steel was just something useful as turnover, to be bought as cheaply and sold as expensively as possible. The world was changing, the money manipulators were rapidly becoming more important and influential than those responsible for production and development. Perhaps in the early 1970s, too many Sheffielders had forgotten that business was about only one thing and that was profit.

A chance conversation with one of the companies to whom Rotherham Tinsley sold scrap, reawakened all the memories of the merchanting trade. The casual offer of a cup of tea and a chat about the future, saw me quickly giving notice to Rotherham. I left on the day the merger with Brown Bayley was officially announced and realised that I had not discussed salary with my new employers, such was the charm of the Managing Director. A well-respected and very convivial self-made man, who had learned the scrap business at Cox & Danks, he claimed to have had as hard a war as anyone. Finding himself in a reserved occupation, ensured that he had become the resident drinking partner for all his friends, and their comrade-in-arms who had come on leave expecting a wild time...which he endeavoured to provide. His graphic tales of wild nights with Canadian air crew, made a 30 year old listen in awe and even envy.

One of his great beliefs was that, '*ideas are a dime a dozen; good ones though cost a great deal more*'. Yet despite the certainty his knowledge gave him as to the real cost of business success, he would continue looking for the good ideas that would make him rich without risking too much of his wealth. His was the search of a latter-day alchemist: somewhere there existed a scheme that would enable scrap to be converted into wealth without recourse to any capital investment. One such typical scheme attempted to turn a high speed steel grinding residue into a resaleable product. This oily, grey-coloured sludge was deposited by the tool manufacturer into a skip which, when filled, was returned the 15 or so miles to our scrap yard. It was noticed that oil always lay on top of the sludge and it was therefore agreed to take the skip for a trip every day. As each day passed, more and more oil was removed from the top of the skip. Several months, and many miles later, it was decided that no more oil could be removed and the second stage of the plan could be commenced. The sludge consisted of 6/5/2 high speed steel grindings and, if it were premelted to give a known analysis, would be quite valuable. Samples of the 'dry' sludge were shown to a number of local works to see if they would melt the residue. Finally Jessop-Savile agreed to have a go. The resulting explosion ensured that the experiment was never repeated, at least with such a primitive method for removing oil. The resulting premelts also had the interesting attribute of being so heavily contaminated by grinding by-products, with not only a high silicon content, but also high sulphur levels that they fitted no known specification. Were these the first 'free-cutting high speed steels'? Whatever, no-one wanted to buy them and they were eventually sold at a substantial financial deficit and no small loss of face.

The scrap and reusable trades are an undeniable necessity to the steel industry. They help keep costs down and ensure a high proportion of metal is recycled. Long before recycling and 'green' issues became a popular concern, the metal industries had been widely practising it. As early as 2000 BC, the archeological record provides evidence for such recycling with scrap bronze axe heads being remelted. No doubt they were collected and sold on by some Bronze Age scrap merchant!

The steelworks naturally found it impractical to deal with dozens of small scrap gatherers and would only deal with the larger companies; effectively creating a two tier trade. Each of the large works issued 'labels' or permits to the suppliers for whatever category of scrap they were requiring and these were allocated out to the many small companies, who in turn delivered on behalf of the big dealers. The mixing of inferior grades of scrap was with some scrap dealers, an established practice, almost an art form and was the source of the occasional fraud trial. Nobody openly condoned the practice, but it was an easy way to make some money...until you were caught and even then it was not unknown for someone else to take the 'rap' on another's behalf, one assumes for a consideration.

It was very important to an aspiring steel merchant to acquire a

Hagah the Bronze Age scrapman.

range of contacts, and was especially important to have them with the departments responsible for disposing of surplus or semi-defective steels, especially at British Steel Corporation. Not only were they the country's biggest steel manufacturer, they also produced the most surpluses, the most seconds. Consequently their lists were among the most difficult to obtain! The early 1970s saw the establishment of many small stockholding and merchanting companies, both in Sheffield and in the Midlands. Trade was buoyant as also was inflation. The Labour Government elected in February 1974 added to the inflationary tendencies of the period by their March budget, which amongst other measures, imposed large increases in steel prices in order to reduce the amount of subsidy the Exchequer was doling out to the British Steel Corporation. A period of high profits as a result of the increased value of stock saw many of these new companies make rapid strides toward becoming financially sound and well established. Increased domestic prices also signalled an opportunity for some of these companies to reduce their dependence on the surplus arisings from the Corporation and to substitute imports which were now available and offered a sound business prospect.

The 1970s will perhaps largely be remembered as a decade of industrial unrest which depending on individual outlook, either created or was driven by inflationary pressures. The steel industry was not exempt from these national trends, although by comparison with most other major industries, its strike record was exemplary as was its general attitude toward industrial relations. 1974 saw the steel and associated companies locally employing 196,800 people and steel production reaching 2,019,800 ingot tons annually. These were happy days indeed, so long as personal income was increasing at a higher level than was the cost of living. The Corporation continued to produce enormous losses, imports of all manner of steel types increased and yet it was still in short supply. These were perhaps more truthfully very strange days. Personal fortunes were made, with swimming pools becoming a reality and individuals replacing their Hillman Hunters with Jaguars. The merchanting trade in particular and the steel industry in general was starting to live in a 'fool's paradise'.

Entertaining of customers and suppliers was carried out on a lavish scale, with companies vying one with the other over the scale and range of gifts which were dispensed, especially at Christmas. Some companies actively discouraged their staff from accepting such gifts, but inevitably the intended recipient's home address would be made known and the present would cunningly be so directed. Needless to say a range of special 'thank you's', would be arranged for those very important people...those who disposed of the surpluses and were responsible indirectly for the new-found wealth of the upcoming generation of Sheffield's Grammar School steel merchants.

Inevitably there were times when surpluses and seconds were insufficient to meet demand. The prospect of buying anything other than seconds from British Steel Corporation was daunting. They, together with the remaining private sector works, seemingly operating an unofficial policy of discouraging the seconds merchants and by so doing they encouraged imports. Stainless, tool steels as well as the more common alloys and carbon steels, had in the UK, a highly priced market. By aligning with the Corporation's published prices, the continental mills found a market which could be exploited and more importantly, they now had a host of small independent merchants and stockholders who were more than willing to help them, so bad was their perception of the Corporation and its dealings.

The Corporation though were doing the same themselves throughout much of Europe. They were increasing their export market share by undercutting prices, to the extent that even the Italians were crying foul at perceived dumping. With losses continuing to be made by the Corporation, and with a glut of imports, the 'fools' paradise' that the steel industry had become could not continue for much longer.

Not only were the British Steel Corporation actively discouraging the new breed of small, young and dynamic merchants, but they were at the same time starting a programme of acquiring their own stockholders. (This would lead to customers having to depend upon a small number of stockholders, many of whom had close links or indeed were owned by British Steel Corporation).

Others in an endeavour to compete, were selling imported steel. The results were obvious. British Steel Corporation started refusing to quote some merchants for steel that was destined for export, on the grounds that they had their own agent in that country and only enquiries routed via their agents would be dealt with. This, of course, flew in the face of common sense, let alone sound business judgement. Over the years, like all social happenings and business is a social happening, at least at a certain level, relationships develop. These may revolve around shared interests...golf, music, religion, even a shared sense of humour. Because of this, despite claims to the contrary, business is not always done on the cheapest prices. Sometimes where a contract may be placed in the end, is decided by who you like most. Such was the case with a Chicago based company, whose purchasing executive found he could not do business with the Corporation's agent. As an old friend, he asked if he could route his enquiries through our company. No amount of trying to reason with the Corporation would get them to amend their position. The result was that the UK received no further enquiries and consequently no orders from that source. The unwordly and inept attitude that this example illustrates, was unfortunately not an isolated one and was symptomatic of the British Steel Corporation at its worst.

Domestically, they had been able to alter much of the market's shape, despite an increasing level of imports and a viable independent sector, they were still in an all-powerful position. There were a few sectors within the industry where they were not even represented and Sheffield was central within these fields. Most notably were the sectors of high speciality; tool steels, some grades of stainless and heat-resisting steels, in addition to a whole range of forged products, special profiles and bright drawn bars. For some of these products however, the independent producer was reliant upon the British Steel Corporation, for the raw material with which to manufacture his finished product and as they began to rationalise and narrow their product range, so began the slow strangulation of these producers. For example, small section billets became almost impossible to obtain. Minimum supply quantities became bigger. Some qualities would only be made if a cast quantity were ordered and this might be 120 tons! As a result, many items which had been profitably produced in the past for the benefit of supplier and customer, became impossible to manufacture in the most efficient manner. Whole ranges and sizes became unobtainable and the impact upon the manufacturing sector was severe. Product lines which had traditionally been profitably manufactured were suddenly priced out of the market. One large manufacturer of edge tools, in an effort to minimise the effects upon their business, went so far as to build their own rolling mill and find their own billets. Few though were in a position to do this and the decline in many traditional engineering companies may be traced back to the monopolistic attitude which the Corporation fostered at this time.

Chapter Eleven

D'AVIGNON, DOWNSIZING AND DOOM

THE INDEPENDENT STEEL PRODUCERS had been reacting to changing domestic and international markets with a series of mergers, which had the effect of rationalising output and consequently reducing employment. One early merger which had included the nascent British Steel Corporation, was the creation in 1969 of Sheffield Rolling Mills, whose constituent parts were the Corporation itself with 45% of the shares, Balfour Darwins with 38% and James Neill Holdings, owning the remaining 17%. The new company controlled the works of Sheffield Forge and Rolling Mills, Andrews-Toledo, Hallamshire Steel and File and the very modern ex-English Steel Corporation bar mill at Tinsley Park, which was now a part of British Steel Corporation. In 1971, prior to acquiring Rotherham-Tinsley Steels, Brown Bayleys Steels had made an unsuccessful attempt to acquire the new company, but in the event, the private sector shareholding was sold out in 1974 to the Corporation and the eventual closure of the older plants became a certainty.

The area's biggest private sector employers, Firth Brown, themselves became the target for the acquisitive breed of financiers. Dunford and Elliot's approaches were rejected but eventually Jessel and his other steel company, Richard Johnson & Nephew emerged as winners. The new company, to be known as Johnson Firth Brown had a turnover of £100 million per annum and were by any standards a major international force... but not for long.

The same year, 1973, saw Dunford Elliot planning to merge with the area's last remaining large independent steel producer - Brown Bayley Steels. They were at that stage, effectively controlled by the Department of Trade & Industry, through the Industrial Reorganisation Corporation, who controlled 50.8% of the Ordinary share capital. The Government raised no objections and, in early 1974, there began the last decade of Sheffield as a significant and distinctly steel city. The long-term effects of overmanning, insufficient capital investment, a business philosophy of demanding instant gratification, together with strong world competition would combine to provide fertile ground for a future Government to invoke *'laissez-faire'* and use that to justify the industry's demise. The good trading years of the early 1970s had missed the incumbents at Leeds Road.

As their new owners were to remark,

'Brown Bayley were virtually bankrupt. Despite full order books, they had contrived to lose in the first 6 months of 1973, a figure of £233,000. In the same period, Dunford Hadfields had made a profit of £2,287,000. Rotherham-Tinsley though had made a profitable contribution'.

The newly merged company would employ 6,550 people and had assets in excess of £18 million and was born at a time of exceptional demand for steel. The new Chairman, Peter Edwards, justified the merger with the usual statement which identified the, *'much wider product range and production facilities which would make them more effective in international competition, particularly in the Common Market'.* He also recognised the opportunities which the period's trading conditions offered.

'In the current boom conditions, with both companies fully stretched in meeting extremely strong order books, there could be immediate benefits from working together.'

As in almost all mergers of the period, the new owners were at lengths to assure their employees that job security existed.

'Both companies are short of labour and even if cyclical downturn comes, there is the home area to attack which is currently supplied by imports.'

Despite the 'hiccups' at Leeds Road, the future augured well for the new group which had clearly identified its priorities.

Within one year, Dunford Hadfields had disposed of the 10½ inch mill at Greasboro Street, which Jessel had earlier closed as an economy measure. The mill was bought by Neepsend Rolling Mills who, in an attempt to rationalise some of their own assortment of rolling mills tried to make a success of it, with very mixed results. The rest of the Greasboro Road site was disposed of in 1977 when Spencer Clarke Metal Industries themselves a result of an earlier merger, between two old Sheffield companies, Geo Clarke and Walter Spencer, bought the site and its equipment from Dunford Hadfields. With this purchase the remains of Rotherham Forge's hard-earned trade, passed into yet another set of owners. Rotherham Forge's original site at Forge Lane, was sold to River Don Stampings and would not be redeveloped until 1983 when Hillards opened a supermarket. With the Forge's closure on 27 November 1981, over 200 years of industrial working on the unique island site came to an end and the last 45 workers were made redundant.

Steel-making capacity within Europe continued to expand and the manifest crisis was appreciated with the recognition that the steel works within the Community could produce 1,000 million tons of annual supply, but had only 700 million tons of foreseeable demand. Commissioner D'Avignon, was therefore instructed to formulate a scheme for reducing the supply side of the steel industry. The simple answer was to institute plant closures and to insist that national governments ceased subsidising their industries. Unfortunately for the British Steel Industry, this policy change more or less coincided with the Election of a new Conservative Government, whose leadership had very definite views about the country's reliance on the old smoke stack industries and was determined to radically change the industrial face of the nation while at the same time destroying the power bases of the Unions, who had been such a cause of anguish to the previous Conservative administration. The Corporation was at that stage losing £1 million a day despite having shed 100,000 jobs nationally in the previous 5 years. Clearly the steel industry would be a prime target for the new administration, especially as there was the added bonus of all their actions in downsizing, the industry was being seen as a part of a European-wide problem... it would almost be a '*force majeure*'. The Commission's proposals were welcomed by the British Government and they set about emasculating the industry in the interests of necessity. Steel and its associated industries were to be decimated and the future prosperity of whole communities placed in jeopardy.

The appointment of Ian McGregor, as Chairman of the Corporation, signalled the beginning of the Government campaign. The unions did not lie down and wait to be offered as a sacrificial offering to the god of market forces. A national strike was called by the British Iron & Steel Trades Confederation, a union which in the past had always acted with much responsibility, in an effort to defend jobs. The strike, which officially only involved the Corporation's employees, naturally spilled over to affect workers in the private sector, notably those at Hadfields. Here some of the striking steel workers had invited local branches of the National Union of Mineworkers to join their picket lines. This they did and as a result, their actions were used by the Government to portray the NUM as a Union which was meddling in matters not of its concern. The strike, which lasted from January to April 1980, was the signal for a rash of closures, starting with Bilston works which gave notice of closure within weeks of the strike being settled.

The initial effects within Europe of the D'Avignon agreement was in complete contrast to those in the UK. Steel-making capacity would increase in West Germany by 15%; in Italy by 41%, whilst the UK saw a reduction of 16%. Similarly, the UK suffered 45% of all the job losses, whilst Italy's share amounted to only 5%. Our European partners were acting with their own national interests at heart, in contrast to the British Government who welcomed the possibility of shedding jobs and creating a more compliant labour force, which was considered a necessity in post-industrial Britain.

Government anti-inflationary policies also created severe economic depression. By 1982, industrial output was running at a rate of 20% less than 1979. In the same period, investment had fallen by a staggering 36%. The magazine *British Business*, published in January 1983, featured figures indicating the decline in demand for steel. They make little sense, unless viewed against the background of the aim of deliberate de-industrialisation being a Government policy.

Industry	Down by
Railways	43.2%
Shipbuilding	10.5%
Construction	9.4%
Electrical Engineering	31.7%
Mechanical Engineering	20.1%
Motor vehicles	10.4%
Hollowware	20.5%
Wire Products	21.4%
All others	14.7%
Average	19.4%

Historically, steel had always been one of the first industries to feel the effects of economic recession, but this recession saw little attempt at mitigating its long-term effects. There was a strange feeling of finality which permeated the trade. Who would be the next to go? The large scale reduction in demand affected the entire industry from the bulk steel producing British Steel Corporation, down to the small independent specialist producers of which Sheffield had so many.

Sheffield was going to be badly hit. Alarmingly, as companies closed, they were not mothballed. Rather the equipment was either broken up or sold off and the sites cleared. This was not so much a recession, rather a clearance. Mammon was leaving Vulcan, having found more profitable areas where her devotees could practice their activities. The entrepreneurs that had been attracted to steel in the early 1970s were leaving the, by now, much belittled, smoke stack industries as fast as they could off-load their unsecured loan stocks. All of this was very much in accord with the Government's wishes.

As William the Conqueror had laid waste to the North following 11th Century dissent, so the 20th Century which had spawned the new Conservatism, saw the North being put to the economic sword and its means of economic well-being seriously reduced. By the time of the Election in 1979, steel was already experiencing difficulties and employment was being drastically reduced as a result of modern and less labour intensive production methods. The widespread introduction of Basic Oxygen steelmaking and Electric Arc melting had revolutionised the practices of steelmaking; larger quantities, using fewer men could be produced in a much shorter time. Bigger furnaces were linked with the development of continuous casting, a technique largely developed in Sheffield. This would further revolutionise the manning levels of the industry, effectively eliminating as it did the need for billet and blooming mills. The science of metallurgy had developed steels, which were capable of exhibiting similar properties to some of the highly alloyed ones in general use, without the need to use expensive alloying elements.

Parallel developments had produced steels which did not require heat treatment, yet these forging steels incorporated the required physical properties upon cooling and thus avoided the expense of a time-consuming extra heat-treatment. All these developments together with materials and methods substitution, were leading to a large scale erosion of the local industry's ability to sustain the massive reliance upon it for wealth creation, which had been its role for over a century.

Since 1971, the Sheffield area had already lost 16,000 jobs by this erosion. The neo-liberalist policies adopted by the Conservative government, turned this decline into a headlong rush into the unknown territory of de-industrialising whole communities. 1980 saw the Corporation announce the loss of 3,400 jobs. 1982 saw the Corporation account for the following local job losses: 650 at Tinsley Park and Stocksbridge; 633 at their Stainless Division; 275 at River Don, and at the end of the year an additional 1,709 redundancies were made at Rotherham, Stocksbridge and Tinsley Park Works.

By 1983, contraction was in full spate, with the following job losses announced: Aurora Steels (a creation by conglomerating the steel

The site of Tinsley's 10″ mill as it is today.

interests of Edgar Allen, Balfour Darwins and Osborn Steels), 1,550; Neepsend Steels 860; J J Habershon 200; James Neill 188; Effingham Steelworks 82; Spencer Clarke 162; Sanderson Kayser 286; Shardlows 233: Tinsley Wire 500; Daniel Doncaster 837; Arthur Lee 1,000. Local companies financial results were a reflection of the job cuts which desperate companies had been forced to take in an effort to remain solvent. Arthur Lee reported a loss of £3,187,000. Spencer Clarke a loss of £629,000. Neepsend a loss of £1,660,000. Aurora a loss of £5,240,000 and British Steel Corporation a loss of £358,000,000.

Woodhouse and Rixson had produced a creditable profit of £607,000.

Additionally the Government, who had dogmatically rejected any form of subsidy to help the industry, was responsible for encouraging a number of 'reshaping' reports, paid for out of public funds, which further exacerbated the position by recommending even more cuts.

Amongst these reshaping and rationalising reports were those produced by Lazards, affecting the castings provisions of British Steel Corporation's River Don and Renishaw Works as well as Holbrook Precision Castings. This would cost 2,000 jobs. Another report, this time dealing with restructuring of the tool steel industry which was in effect produced by The Bank of England, would be responsible for a 50% reduction in overall capacity and the loss of 14,000 jobs, amongst them some of those mentioned in the previous chapter. Action taken on the findings of a series of 'Phoenix' reports, would eventually ensure the total collapse of the remaining traditional type of steelmaking business which had sustained the city for over a century. Hadfields, which by 1983 was in the ownership of the multi-national 'Lonhro' Group, had already shed 2,700 jobs and under Phoenix 2, the new owners sold out their majority shareholding to a consortium of alloy steel producers in which British Steel Corporation and Guest, Keen and Nettlefold were the dominant forces. The plant finally closed with the loss of the last 700 jobs in October 1983 and with this closure, the last steel bars were also rolled at the old Wharf Lane works of Dyson Shirt & Co.

Remains of Tinsley's sheet mill site as nature re-states her claim on the land.

What remains of Tinsley's 12″ Mill following demolition.

The subsidies received by our European competitors were of course hidden; they emerged in the form of cheaper energy costs, cheaper transport costs, cheaper employment costs, not to be confused with the actual wages, where British wage rates for steelworker were the lowest in Western Europe. At the same time, considerably higher levels of funding for research and development were available to our European competitors.

Clearly though, the British Steel Corporation, which was still losing money at an alarming rate, was a perhaps fortunate demonstration and proof for the government that subsidies did not work. Nonetheless Government would not be persuaded to alter its position. Steel must go, but shareholders must be protected from the real economic chill. It has been suggested that all the Government did was to speed up an inevitable process and that it was foresight on their part by 'grasping the nettle', which the downsizing of the industry presented. By their actions, the painful process was concentrated into a relatively short transition period and left the labour force to suffer the real pain of adjustment relatively unaided. Later events in Europe would seem to confirm this view. A Government which denied subsidies and withdrew industrial support, nevertheless thoroughly embraced the concept of providing ample assistance to compliant companies; similarly groups of shareholders who accepted the schemes for contraction and closure, were treated with greater consideration. Generally these schemes and others affecting many similar industries were known as 'rationalisation'.

The 1982 *Industry Act* granted £22 million, later increased to £36 million, to assist private sector companies to 'contract and consolidate'. The British Steel Corporation had no such problems with shareholders and by the time Ian McGregor left in mid 1983, the workforce had already been reduced by half from its 1979 figure and their market share had continued to decline as, to be fair, did their losses. These had been cut from a high point of £9 million a week down to £2 million a week. Total losses accruing to the Corporation during the period of McGregor's control were some £2.4 BILLION! Yet so delighted were the Government with his performance that he and his company were paid performance related bonuses.

As early as 1972, the British Steel Corporation had entered into an agreement with Firth Brown, to exchange certain fixed assets and products which cost the Corporation a lump sum balancing figure of £2½ million. This early attempt to bring some rationale into an area which would have been best not to have become a part of a state-owned steel industry, would be the forerunner of a much larger and wider ranging rationalisation exercise in the last years of steel.

The effects of the Government sponsored Phoenix 3 plan combined the forging and drop-forging interests of British Steel Corporation's River Don Works together with those of Johnson Firth Brown. This was funded to the extent of a £40 million lump sum from public funds. Somewhat surprisingly, the whole of Johnson Firth Brown, including the very profitable areas not included in the merger, could have been purchased on the stock market for only £14 million...for such was the stock market's valuation of the company which had lost £15 million, in the previous 18 months trading. Alongside this it was estimated that River Don had lost around £30 million in the past decade.

The company born out of the ashes of two of the area's biggest employers, would be known as Sheffield Forgemasters. They would be a 'formidable production unit capable of competing profitably in

Firth Brown's Gate. A reminder of past glories photographed in 1999. This gate is now part of a modern industrial estate in the east end of Sheffield.

international markets in which demand had continued to fall'. The merger was completed after 'cautious and delicate negotiations'. It was anticipated that they would need to employ some 4,000 people, which meant that an initial 1,100 jobs would go. Johnson Firth Brown and British Steel Corporation would own the new company on an equal basis - JFB would transfer £61m of assets from which £20m would be deducted to meet bank debt. Included within these assets was the new £12.5m precision forging plant, only recently commissioned by Johnson Firth Brown. British Steel Corporation transferred to Johnson Firth Brown some £41m of assets, including an all important £17m in cash.

In the three years to the end of 1982 a total of 20,000 steelworking jobs had been lost in Sheffield.

The city had 40,000 unemployed, which generated an unemployment rate of 13.9% compared with the national figure of 9.5%. The President of the Independent Steel Makers Association, BISPA, Peter W Lee reported,

'The damage that has been done (to the industry) cannot be reversed, but for those that remain, these recent events are an element of

hopefulness ... The fact that we are still here is, in itself a matter of satisfaction ... although there have been some grievous casualties ... Over the last year or two, private sector steel in Sheffield had suffered very greatly as a result of subsidised competition from British Steel Corporation and European producers. The physical effects of this are obvious to anyone who travels to the East End of the City and the human hardship is a matter with which we are all personally acquainted in one way or another'.

May 1984 saw the end of bulk steel making on the site of Johnson Firth Brown, all melting being transferred under the terms of the merger to the River Don Works. A visit in 1984 to Southern Germany saw an amazed German telling a Sheffield Steel Company Director,

'You are the richest nation in Europe. You are built on coal, surrounded by fish and oil, you are all educated. Only the British could afford to have so many people made out of work'.

Chapter 12

STREAMLINED - LEANER AND FITTER

'Sheffield is passing through what is probably the most traumatic and testing period in its history as an industrial centre. The City has been particularly badly hit, because of its dependence upon steel and its related industries and we have been more badly hit than many outsiders realise.' (Sheffield Chamber of Commerce, *'Quality of Sheffield'*, January 1983.)

A ONCE PROUD CITY HAD SEEN its primary means of economic success, reduced to a fraction of what it once was and all in less than 10 years. Household names had ceased to exist except as memories and the demolition men were moving in to clear the sites and create a series of 1980s style bomb sites, complete with fireweed and other assorted wildlife. Road haulage companies ceased trading as did chip shops, corner shops, pubs and clubs. Similarly small engineers and furnace builders suffered in the industrial wasteland that Sheffield had become. The City was in decline industrially and the cement which had held communities together was similarly showing distinct signs of deterioration, with old and young alike suffering the pain of being casualties in an economic war which was being fought without any rules of engagement and with one side only having weapons available to them!

Even now, some 15 years after Sheffield Chamber of Commerce

Millsands, site of Sheffield Forge and Rolling Mills, 1999.

A part of Avesta Sheffield's works, 1999.

wrote so truthfully, the City continues to suffer. Some city centre areas still to have an unemployment rate in excess of 20%, while the skills developed to serve the steel industry, have been less than easy to transfer to others. The streamlined, leaner and fitter rump steel industry continues to operate in the area and quite successfully, though it is still susceptible to the vagaries of international trading conditions. The old British Steel Corporation are melting, rolling and casting at Stocksbridge, Renishaw, Aldwarke, Thrybergh and Roundwood. Now, safely in the private domain and known as British Steel PLC, they widely publicise the statistic that they locally produce more steel than the City ever did, using the most modern equipment and with a fraction of the manpower. This is an undoubted achievement. They do of course achieve this by concentrating upon only segments of the markets which were once served by the industry's combined productive capacity, with its range and variety, which the steelworks of the City could previously offer.

From the smallest to the largest sizes in a myriad of shapes and qualities, the steel companies within the area had contrived to meet an ever-expanding market not only for variety but also for the economy of working the steel to produce finished goods. Sheer volume and the integrity of the product may have been maintained and indeed improved, but it is an illusion to suggest that the city is still meeting the same demands...for it is now simply incapable of doing so.

British Steel PLC continue working at their various plants, but in line with international trading conditions in the steel industry, redundancies continue to be made with the persistent demand to reduce operating costs. Most notably, Templeboro Rolling Mills has closed, while this book has been in the final stages of preparation.

The stainless division of British Steel was merged with the Swedish Group, Avesta AB, in 1992 and the new Anglo-Swedish company, with its headquarters in Stockholm, became a subsidiary of British Steel PLC in 1995, with British Steel holding 51% of the shares of Avesta Sheffield. In Sheffield, they operate the Shepcote Lane, Cyclops and Alloy Steel Rod plants. The company is a world leading manufacturer and supplier of stainless steels which are produced by the latest methods and technology, including Stainless Melting and Continuous Casting (SMACC) with a melting capacity in excess of 500,000 tonnes of stainless steel a year. Much of the UK's stainless steel scrap is recycled in this plant and even the dust particles which occur as part of the fumes produced in the melting process, are themselves recycled in a specially-designed furnace which converts the dust into metal, containing such valuable alloying elements as nickel and chromium. The Coil Products Division operates the largest single stainless steel finishing facility in Europe, having opened in 1991 at a total cost of £35 million. It is complemented by a fully automated storage and stock retrieval system.

Worldwide, the Company employs around 7,500, with just over 2,000 UK employees. Adverse trading conditions and the high value of Sterling, have forced them to review their position and this will shortly involve yet more job shedding and closures. The decision of both the British and Swedish Governments not to embrace the Euro in the first wave is, the Company argues, adversely affecting them.

Phoenix 3, which created Sheffield Forgemasters has produced a company which, after suffering some unwanted publicity over its alleged involvement with the so called Iraqi Super Gun Affair, appeared to want to operate in a very unpublicised manner. They are still undoubtedly a world force in their sector of the industry, but employ only a fraction of those who originally worked for the constituent companies. Pleasingly, they have entered into some of the spirit of Sheffield's regeneration and the now 'cleaned-up' River Don offices and surroundings are a great improvement and a credit to the Company, which is currently American controlled.

Of the several smaller companies who continue working within the local steel industry, perhaps Spartan Steels' attitude to their current position, a decade or so since the devastation of the industry, says it all...'the good news is that we are still here'!

They have found niche markets and in the old traditions of the City's steel industry, these are all highly specialised and with a high added value, having been ignored by the larger producers.

Aurora Metals, having shed during the 1980s many hundreds of jobs and suffered plant closures, including that of Osborn Steels in Ecclesfield, which when first opened was described as the largest specialist steelmaking plant in Britain, was taken over by the Australian Group, Australian National Industries Ltd. They still maintain a significant manufacturing base in the area.

Rotherham Forge's old site at Greasboro Street in Rotherham still echoes to the distinctive sound of traditional hot 'metal bashing'. Their much reduced labour force and plant are still rolling Beater Bars and other traditional lines, but the bulk of the business is now concentrated on a much more sophisticated range of metals and end products which the old company could never have dreamt of. Nickel, cobalt and titanium alloys as well as alloy and stainless steels are now rolled for among others, the aerospace market, in the form of special and standard sections and sheet, they complement the aluminium-bronze and other 'super-clean' alloys which the company produces for the construction, nuclear and conventional power generation industries world-wide. Their mills are now dedicated to being much more flexible.

Being quite capable of not only rolling orders of several hundred tonnes, but also accepting lots down to 100 kilogrammes or even smaller. In markets where customers are unwilling to finance stock of high value materials, this ability to work with the customer is an undoubted improvement upon some of the old 'like it or lump it' attitudes, which historically permeated much of the industry. Greasboro Street now has a modern dedicated on-site laboratory, which enables their products to be released with full quality certification - again a far cry from the rather humble facilities with which Rotherham Forge was previously equipped.

The surviving companies have been forced to adapt to new situations and also adopt new and sometimes strange and certainly untraditional, practices. A greater awareness of the absence of 'jobs for life' affects the district's remaining 30,000 or so workers who have found that Vulcan still has a place for them. There is also an air of confidence that having survived the traumas of the 1980s, the industry is capable of reinventing itself, although in common with all the traditional industries which helped shape this century, no-one would conceive of any of them ever being able to generate employment to the same extent as in the past.

The city then is still looking for new forms of inward investment and perhaps new forms of entrepreneurship. Hopefully less dependent upon the whims and fancies of the Stock Market, as personified by speculative international investors who have the power to affect so many lives and communities. Sheffield's environment was a major casualty of the City's industrial success and

Three views of Five Weirs Walk, views around Washford Bridge.

it is perhaps fitting that with the failure of its major industry, the local environment has started to recover, aided by a higher level of public awareness and concern for conservation and environmental issues.

The Loxley Valley, once the home of a number of small rolling mill companies now lies silent. The mills have gone, the demolition contractors removed anything of value and have left the valley to its little river, its fish and birdlife. Similar happenings can be observed along the Five Weirs Walk, constructed through some of the old centres of Sheffield's steelworking. The water quality of the River Don is now sufficiently improved that it sustains fish and other aquatic life. Childhood dreams of fishing in the Don are now a reality, as also is being able to boat down Sheffield's canal without feeling that one was commuting along an open sewer. Improved water quality, and its ability to sustain life may have been in the longer term achieved by legislation, but the prime mover in these environmental improvements has been the industrial desolation which has seen the river system change from among the most heavily polluted in the Western hemisphere, into areas which with appropriate landscaping are truly pleasant and accessible for recreation.

Recreation, in its many forms, is one area which the City is exploring in its drive for regeneration and the authorities can point to some notable achievements in this field. Perhaps the most obvious one was the opening on 4 September 1990, of the Meadowhall Shopping Centre, occupying 1.5 million sq ft of the derelict site of Dunford Hadfields Steelworks. The Centre annually draws over 30 million shoppers and visitors to its many delights, not least of which is the larger than life bronze representation of a 3-man team of crucible steel melters at work. A memento of what used to be done, with such effort, on a site now dedicated to the generation of profit by less physically demanding means. The Centre employs at peak times, directly and indirectly, some 15,000 people, and, as such, provides more employment than the old Dunford Hadfields works did, almost certainly at an enhanced profit margin.

The World Student Games held in the City in 1991 was heralded by national opinion as a serious mistake, for which the City had mortgaged its future. The provision of such world-class sporting centres as the Stadium, the Arena and the Swimming Centre at Ponds Forge, have heralded the beginnings of the City as a centre of sporting excellence. The dereliction and contamination which the closure of Brown Bayley's works on Leeds Road left have been swept

Don Valley Bowl and Stadium as seen from the viewing platform. (see opposite)

away, and modern state-of-the-art facilities for sport and entertainment which are in great demand, have replaced the works. Perhaps the number of full-time jobs, these facilities have helped create is relatively small. Nonetheless, they are significant, as the City has received approval, together with funding, for its future role as the centre for the United Kingdom Sports Institute.

Sheffield now has its badly needed airport, partly built on the reclaimed site of ESCs 1960s 'Tinsley Park Steel Works', as well as a modern, high-intensity, rapid transit transport system in the shape of Supertram. Also a range of facilities, including modern hotels and a revived Canal Basin, all of which, only 30 years ago, were not even dreams. The City, of which it used to be said fell asleep at 10.30 pm, is now recognised as a leading provider of nightlife and entertainment and is actively developing an infrastructure, especially in the Cultural Industries Quarter, to support this new industry. The National Centre for Popular Music, which opened on 1 March 1999, is a visual statement of the City's approach to an economy which no longer relies upon manufacturing for its prosperity and is actively encouraging the city centre establishment of these new cultural

Don Valley, Sheffield Arena.

A steel works vessel, now used as a viewing platform, Don Valley Bowl.

Sheffield City airport, showing arrival of an internal commuter flight. The service complex has been extended since photographed.

industries and giving support to their entrepreneurs. This option is not a 'quick fix' solution, but part of a bid to build a multi-faceted future for the 'City of Steel', which so nearly came to total grief as a result its reliance upon one industry.

The Heart of the City project, which when completed at a cost of £120m, will show to the world at large the face of a revived and vigorous community with aptitudes and skills no longer limited to 'metal bashing'. This will give Sheffield a new start in the next Millennium, when the pain and traumas of the last 20 years have subsided and the City which developed all the skills required for steelmaking, will have found a new and equally significant role.

Memories of Sheffield's metal bashing days. A silent reminder of the past. The huge drop forge frame which once beat out vital components for use in war and peace, now stand mute at the junction of Saville Street East and Sutherland Street, Sheffield.

Chapter 13

A List Of Some Local Steel Companies That Have Ceased Trading Since 1960

Just Some of the local Steel Companies that have ceased trading since 1960:

The Crucible Steel Co
R Denton Steel & Tool Co Ltd
Dunford & Elliott (Sheffield) Ltd
Engineering Steels Co Ltd
Thos Firth & John Brown Ltd *
Jos Gillott & Sons Ltd
J J Habershon & Sons Ltd
Hobson Houghton & Co Ltd
Jonas & Colver (Novo) Ltd
Montgomery Skinner Ltd
Wm Moore & Co
B K Morton & Co Ltd
Muxlow & Knott Ltd
The Park Gate Iron & Steel Co Ltd #
The Sheffield Hollow Drill Steel Co Ltd
W H Shephard Ltd
Ashworth Pitt & Co Ltd
Steel Peech & Tozer Ltd #
The Tinsley Rolling Mills Co Ltd
John Vessey & Sons Ltd
Wardlows Ltd
Rotherham Forge & Rolling Mills Co Ltd
Geo Clarke (Sheffield) Ltd
H R Waterfall Barber Ltd
Rotherham Steel Strip Ltd
J Beardshaw & Sons Ltd
Arthur Blackwell & Sons Ltd
Clay Wheels Rolling Mills Ltd
Balfour Darwins Ltd
Osborn Steels Ltd
Denton & Best Ltd
Don Forge & Eng. Ltd
Eaton & Booth (Sheffield) Ltd
Hallamshire Steel & File Co Ltd
Kenyon Bros & Co Ltd

Chas Kenyon & Sons Ltd
Wm Kenyon & Sons (Loxley) Ltd
Neepsend Rolling Mills Ltd
John Holding & Co (1955) Ltd
Niagara Forge Ltd
Wincobank Rolling Mills Ltd
John Wood & Sons (Wisewood) Ltd
English Steel Corporation Ltd #*
Brown Bayley Steels Ltd
Hadfields Ltd
Saml Fox & Co Ltd #
Rotherwood Steel & Eng. Ltd
Swift Bros (Rolling Mills) Ltd
Geo Senior & Co Ltd
W T Flather & Co Ltd
Jessop-Savile Ltd
Annealers Ltd
Baker Bessemer & Co Ltd
Dinnington Steels Ltd
Fesswick Ltd
Apollo Steels Ltd
Effingham Steelworks Ltd
Wm Turner & Sons Ltd
Napier Steels Ltd
Thos C Hurdley (Sheffield) Ltd
Firth Vickers Stainless Steels Ltd
Moss & Gamble Ltd
Ibbotson Bros Ltd
Leadbeater & Scott Ltd
Sheffield Rolling Mills Ltd
Kelham Island Steelworks Ltd
Shalesmoor Steel Ltd
Midland & Low Moor Iron & Steel Co Ltd.

* Parts operate as Sheffield Forgemasters Ltd and associates.
# Parts operate as British Steel PLC

Chapter 14

A Synopsis of Some Major Local Companies 1960 - 1964

Balfour and Darwins Ltd
Capital Steel Works, Sheffield S3
'Trading in the first 4 months has been satisfactory'
Products: *Aircraft Steels; High Speed and Alloy Tool Steels; Nickel and Stainless Steels; Engineers Tools; Magnets; Castings.*

Employees: 1450

Equipment:

Balfours	1 x 2^1/$_2$ ton Electric arc melting furnace
	2 x ^{1}/$_2$ ton High frequency
	1 x 1 ton High frequency
	1 x 10 inch 3 high rolling mill
	2 x 11 inch 2 high rolling mill
	2 x 14 inch 2 high rolling mill
	10 hammers from 5 to 50 cwt
	Heat treatment and finishing plant.
Darwins	5 x electric high frequency furnaces from 80lb to 1 ton
	1 x electric arc 3 ton
Beeley Wood	12 hammers 5 cwt to 4 ton
Andrews Toledo	3 x Acid Open Hearth Furnaces 20-25 ton
	1 x 10 ton electric arc
	5 x rolling mills 8^1/$_2$ inch - 25 inch
	1 x wire rod mill (installed 1958 at a cost of £160,000)
Sheffield Forge	3 x sheet mills 18/20 inch
	8 x bar mills 10/14 inch

Brown Bayley Steels Ltd
'Riverdale', Riverdale Road, Sheffield, S10
'The recession in the Alloy and Special Steel trade persisted for the greater part of the year... I am glad to say the order position today is much more healthy'.

Products: *Billets, bars, forgings in special carbon, alloy and stainless steels. Railway tyres and axles. Stainless steel strip, sheet and castings.*

Employees:	3,000
Equipment:	2 x acid open hearth furnaces 45 ton
	1 x basic open hearth furnace 45 ton
	6 x electric arc furnace 8/24 ton
	2 x high frequency furnace $^1/_2$ ton
Melting Capacity:	135,000 ingot tons per annum
	1 x 27 inch stand reversing mill
	1 x 14 inch billet mill
	3 x bar mills 9 inch - 10$^5/_8$ inch
	1 x cold sheet mill
	3 x narrow strip mills
	1 x tyre mill
	2 x ring rollers
	4 x presses 500-1,500 ton
	8 x horizontal forging machines
	12 x hammers $^1/_2$ ton -7 ton
	plus heat treatment and finishing plant

English Steel Corporation Ltd
River Don Works, Sheffield
Extracts from Chairman's remarks:

> '1964 opened with an increased volume of orders... Most of our plant should work at a more satisfactory level through the year... In recent months, however, there has been substantial increases in salaries, wages, electricity and rates, which cannot be recovered in selling prices, which indeed have themselves been recently reduced'.

Products: *Billets 2-6 inch; Blooms 6-24 inch; Rounds $^7/_{16}$ inch-1 inch dia; flats $1^1/_4$ inch-8 inch wide x $^1/_4$-$^1/_2$ coil; $^7/_{16}$ inch-1 inch dia. x 600lbs; Press forgings up to 175 tons; drop forgings up to 1.500 lbs; Cold forgings; Extrusions; Castings up to 185 tons; Heavy rolled plate up to 24 inch thick in carbon and alloy steels: High speed and tool steels.*

Also, Springs, Engineers cutting tools, Magnets, Heavy engineering up to 300 ton in weight and up to 90 inch in length; Railway wheels and axles.

Employees:	13,107
	(inc. those at Manchester and Darlington)
Production 1963:	416,000 ingot tons.
Equipment:	15 x open hearth furnaces 40-90 tons
	9 x electric arc furnace 10-100 tons

6 x electric induction furnace 1-3 ton
1 'Heraus' vacuum melting furnace,
15,000 lbs
1 x 48 inch plate mill
1 x 28 inch blooming mill
1 x 10 inch double duo
1 x 12 inch rod mill
1 x 10 inch rod mill
plus:
Forge, drop forge, spring making plant,
engineers tool making plant, heat treatment
plant and vacuum degassing equipment.

Tinsley Park Development
Greenfield Site: £26/30 million development.
Opened: 15 October 1963

Employees:	1,400
Equipment:	2 x Electric arc 100 ton. 300,000 ton annual capacity
	1 x blooming mill 42 inch x 100 inch, 2 high reversing; 500,000 ton annual capacity
	2 x billet mills 32 inch x 84 inch, 2 high reversing
	1 x bar mill 20 inch, 3 stand, 2 high reversing
	1 x intermediate mill 16 inch, 3 stand, 3 high
	1 x cross country finishing rain 7 x 14/11 inc. vertical and horizontal stands

Thos Firth & John Brown Ltd
Atlas Works, Sheffield S4
Manufacturers of: *carbon and alloy steel billets, slabs, black and bright bars, high speed, carbon and alloy tool steels, die steel, tyres, rings, castings, drop forgings, stampings and heavy engineering.*

Employees:	7,600
Equipment:	5 x Acid open hearth furnaces 50-100 tons capacity
	5 x Electric arc furnaces 14-30 tons capacity
	3 x High frequency furnaces $1/2$ - 6 tons capacity
	Vacuum, consumable arc melting facilities
	1 x cogging mill 28 inch
	1 x finishing mill 26 inch
	3 x bar mills 8-14 inch

Tyre and ring rolling plant
8 presses 600-6,000 ton capacity
7 forging hammers $1/2$-1 ton capacity
Heat Treatment and finishing plant

Also within group:

Firth Vickers Stainless Steels Ltd

1 x cogging mill 18 inch 3 high
1 x bar finishing mill 18 inch
1 x double duo mill $10^1/2$ inch
2 x bar mills 8 inch
6 sheet mills together with associated cold
mill and finishing equipment

Shepcote Lane Rolling Mills

2 x 12 inch cold rolling mills
2 x 10 inch cold rolling mills
2 x 8 inch cold rolling mills
1 x 42 inch hot steckel strip mill and skin
pass, reversing and Senzimir mills

Hadfields Ltd

East Hecla Works, Sheffield S9
Manufacturers of: *wear-resisting, heat-resisting and corrosion-resisting steels. Manganese steel components as well a steelmaking, foundry and forging facilities.*

Employees:	3,800
Equipment:	3 x Open hearth melting furnaces 45-55 ton capacity
	12 x electric arc melting furnaces 4-20 ton capacity
	4 x high frequency furnaces, vacuum melting $1/2$-2 ton capacity
	1 x cogging mill 28 inch
	2 x bar mills 11-14 inch
Forges:	
	2 x 1500-2700 ton capacity
	1 x 800 ton capacity
	1 x 4 ton steam hammer
	8 x pneumatic hammers 5 cwt-2 ton

Steel Foundry:
One of the largest in the world able to produce upward of 600 ton a week with individual weights of 40lb to 40 tons.

Post Script

Since the completion of *Crashing Steel*, the rate of change in the Sheffield steel industry has continued.

The national press of 4 August 1999, revealed that Aurora was to be acquired by the Firth Rixon group. Aurora produce special and high value metals to various industries, including aerospace. The chairman of Firth Rixon indicated that there were likely to be cost savings some £3 million as a result of the merger.

There was no mention of potential job losses.

The last load?